THIS IS PRO BASKETBALL

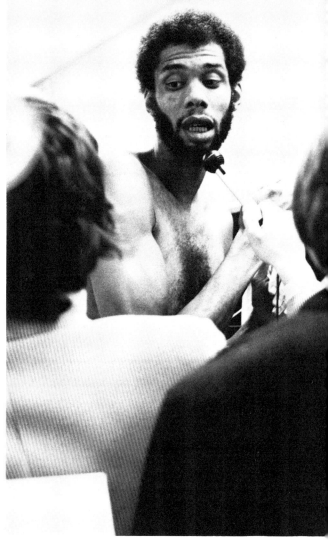

Kareem Abdul-Jabbar, pro basketball's most intimidating force.

THIS IS PRO BASKETBALL

George Sullivan

Illustrated with photographs and diagrams

DODD, MEAD & COMPANY

New York

Library of Congress Cataloging in Publication Data

Sullivan, George, 1927–
     This is pro basketball.

     Includes index.
     SUMMARY: An introduction to the history, rules,
equipment, teams, and well-known players of professional
basketball. Also includes a section of all-time records.
     1.   Basketball—United States—Juvenile literature.
[1.   Basketball]   I.   Title.
GV885.1.S84   796.32'364'0973   77–6497
ISBN 0–396–07455–3

ACKNOWLEDGMENTS

The author is grateful to the many people who helped to make this book possible. Special thanks are offered Lee Williams and June Steitz, Basketball Hall of Fame; Matt Winick and Gail Torres, National Basketball Association; Frank Blauschild, New York Knicks; Tim Simmons, Denver Nuggets; Jim Bukata, New York Nets; Herb Field, Herb Field Art Studio; Gary Wagner, Wagner International Photos; and Bill Brendle, CBS-TV Sports.

CONTENTS

HOW IT BEGAN

- Kareem Abdul-Jabbar—the perfect center, over 7-feet tall, with a well-tapered body and long muscular legs and arms, agile and quick, with speed and finesse. He will take a pass at somewhere near the foul line, throw a head or body fake, and, stretching his long body taut, leap to stuff the ball through the basket. He dribbles and rebounds; he passes and steals. No big man has ever been so versatile.

- Jo Jo White—cool and clever, a playmaker, the game's best fast-breaking guard. He can decide in a millisecond or two whether to stop and shoot or make the final pass to an open man. He can hit from the outside; he can penetrate, accelerating, rocketing past people to leap and score. "There are nights I have to go out and put the ball in the basket," he says, "and there are other nights we have to run more and I'm the quarterback. You go out, you dig, you hustle."

- Julius Erving, Dr. J—pro basketball's Main Man of the 1970s, the most explosive player in the game. He can jump higher than anyone else; he can stay in the air longer. He has speed, quickness, and the ability to shift the ball from one hand to the other hand while in midair and release it from somewhere behind his ear. Most of all, he creates, doing things with a basketball that may never have been seen before. "I believe I can score any time I

Dr. J—Julius Erving—tries a jumper.

want to," Dr. J once said. No one ever contradicted him.

Historians agree that the first professional basketball game was played in 1896 in a Trenton, New Jersey, Masonic Hall. Fred Cooper, the captain of the Trenton team, got $16 for the game, one dollar more than each of his teammates. The first pro basketball league was formed in 1898. Its teams came from the Philadelphia area of Pennsylvania and from Trenton and Camden, New Jersey. The league folded after five years.

From its ragtag beginnings, with competition confined to the northeast corner of the United States, pro basketball has grown into one of the most popular of all American sports. But the game and its trappings are very different from what they were sixty or seventy years ago. A team of the early 1900s might pass the hat among spectators, asking for contributions. Few players were as tall as 6-foot-6. It was a rough-and-tumble game, and players wore hip pads, knee pads, and elbow pads for protection.

Even in recent years, the game has gone through drastic change. There is only one league, not two or more, as was frequently the case. Players are controlled by long-term agreements, not by a league rule that mandates contracts with option-year clauses. There are televised games, more and more of them all the time.

There is one other hallmark of the modern game: players are bigger and stronger, quicker and faster, than ever before. Kareem Abdul-Jabbar, Jo Jo White, and Dr. J are some of the evidence.

This book reviews the history of pro basketball, surveys the game's rules, explains what skills are necessary to be successful, and focuses upon offensive strategy. But always the emphasis is on the players. Pro basketball is a much better game today than it has ever been, and not because of improvements in the playing rules or the use of more sophisticated strategy. The players are the reason.

Basketball is unique because it is a game that was consciously thought up. It did not evolve from existing sports. Football, for example, developed out of soccer and rugby. Baseball is said to have been derived from the English game of rounders.

The man who invented basketball was a young Canadian named James Naismith, an instructor in physical education at the YMCA Training School in Springfield, Massachusetts. He did his inventing in the winter of 1891. His students had become bored with calisthenics, gymnastics, and other indoor athletic activities. The cold weather made it impossible to play baseball, football, or any other outdoor games.

At first Naismith tried adapting football for indoor play, modifying the rules so as to permit tackling only above the hips. He figured that such a

James Naismith, a Canadian by birth, invented the game of basketball.

rule would enable the men to be able to tackle the ball carrier on the hardwood gym floor without hurting him. But the students sneered at the rule. "To ask these men to handle their opponents gently," Naismith wrote, "was to make their favorite sport a laughing stock—and they would have none of it."

Naismith next tried soccer indoors. This was before sneakers had been invented, and the players wore street shoes with soft soles. When attempting to kick the ball, they frequently ended up kicking one another in the shins. "As a result of this," wrote Naismith, "instead of an indoor soccer game, we had a practical lesson in first aid."

Naismith then decided that a wholly new game would have to be developed, one that was easy to learn and could be played by many students. Naismith's first ruling concerning the new game was that it should involve a large ball, a ball the size of a soccer ball. Any sport that depended on a small ball, such as baseball or tennis, also required a hitting instrument of some type, a bat or a racket. Such equipment could make the sport difficult to learn, Naismith reasoned.

Once the type of ball had been settled upon, Naismith turned to the problem of how to advance the ball. He realized he could not permit the players to run with the ball. Running involved tackling, and you could not tackle indoors. The alternative was to allow the ball to be advanced by passing it.

In all existing big-ball games, there was some type of goal over which the ball was carried (as in football or rugby) or driven into (as in soccer or hockey). His game must have a goal, Naismith decided, a boxlike goal at each end of the gym floor. Then he realized that players could prevent the ball from entering the box simply by standing in a semicircle in front of it and blocking it with their bodies. The solution was to elevate the box above the players' heads.

Basket Ball.

The ball to be an ordinary Association foot ball.

1. The ball may be thrown in any direction with one or both hands.

2. The ball may be batted in any direction with one or both hands (never with the fist).

3. A player cannot run with the ball, the player must throw it from the spot on which he catches it, allowance to be made for a man who catches the ball when running at a good speed.

4. The ball must be held in or between the hands, the arms or body must not be used for holding it.

5. No shouldering, holding, pushing, tripping or striking in any way the person of an opponent shall be allowed. The first infringement of this rule by any person shall count as a foul, the second shall disqualify him until the next goal is made, or if there was evident intent to injure the person, for the whole of the game, no substitute allowed.

6. A foul is striking at the ball with the fist, violation of rules 3 and 4, and such as described in rule 5.

7. If either side makes three consecutive fouls it shall count a goal for the opponents (consecutive means without the opponents in the meantime making a foul).

8. A goal shall be made when the ball is thrown or batted *into the basket* from the grounds and stays there, providing those defending the goal do not touch or disturb the goal. If the ball rests on the edge and the opponent moves the basket it shall count as a goal.

9. When the ball goes out of bounds it shall be thrown into the field, and played by the person first touching it. In case of a dispute the umpire shall throw it straight into the field. The thrower in is allowed five seconds, if he holds it longer it shall go to the opponent. If any side presists in delaying the game, the umpire shall call a foul on them.

10. The umpire shall be judge of the men, and shall note the fouls, and notify the referee when three consecutive fouls have been made. He shall have power to disqualify men according to Rule 5.

11. The referee shall be judge of the ball and shall decide when the ball is in play, in bounds, and to which side it belongs, and shall keep the time. He shall decide when a goal has been made, and keep account of the goals with any other duties that are usually performed by a referee.

12. The time shall be two fifteen minutes halves, with five minutes rest between.

13. The side making the most goals in that time shall be declared the winners. In case of a draw the game may, by agreement of the captains, be continued until another goal is made.

First draft of Basket Ball rules. Hung in the gym that the boys might learn the rules — Dec. 1891 James Naismith 6-28-31.

Basketball's thirteen original rules as written by James Naismith in December, 1891.

What to use for goals was the next problem to be solved. "I met Mr. Stebbins, the superintendent of buildings," Naismith wrote, "and I asked him for two boxes about 18 inches square."

Stebbins thought for a minute, then said, "No, I haven't any boxes, but I'll tell you what I do have. I have two old peach baskets in the storeroom."

Naismith asked the superintendent to bring the baskets to the gym. An elevated running track circled the gym floor, forming a balcony. Naismith nailed the baskets to the lower rim of the balcony, one at each end of the gym.

He divided the gym class of 18 men into two nine-man teams. "Throw the ball into the basket," he instructed them.

The playing area was small, 35 by 50 feet (as compared to today's 50 by 94 feet). The players wore long gym pants and long-sleeved jerseys. There was little or no teamwork. As soon as one player gained possession of the ball, all the others would converge upon him. Naismith refereed and seemed to spend all his time either blowing his whistle or shouting, "Pass it! Pass it!" Only one goal was scored.

The game got its name several weeks later when

Frank Mahan, one of the original players, approached Naismith and asked him what he planned on calling it. Naismith had no answer. "Why not call it Naismith ball?" said Mahan. Naismith laughed. "That name would kill any game," he answered.

"Then why not call it basket ball?" said Mahan.

And that's what it came to be called—basket ball. It wasn't until the 1920s that the term began to be used regularly as one word.

The basic principles implied in Naismith's original rules are still in effect. But they have been modified.

For instance, Naismith specified that a player could only advance the ball by throwing it from the spot where he caught it. But this made for a rather stagnant pass-and-catch game. The solution was to permit a player to advance the ball by bouncing it as he ran—to dribble it. Naturally, this speeded up the game considerably.

For a number of years, players were permitted to dribble the ball with both hands. Not until 1898 was the two-handed dribble eliminated.

Naismith's original idea was that teams could be of almost any size, from 3 players to 40. It depended, he said, on the amount of floor space available. A Cornell coach once tried a game with 50 players to a side. The result looked like a subway at rush hour.

Coaches experimented with nine-man, seven-man, and five-man teams. The last named was made mandatory in 1897.

While Naismith's peach baskets eventually gave way to metal rims with cord netting, it didn't happen overnight. By the beginning of basketball's second season, some teams were using cylindrical baskets made of wire mesh. These, like the original peach baskets, had closed bottoms. A small hole in the bottom enabled the referee to poke a stick through and pop the ball out.

A Rhode Island manufacturer introduced a basket with an iron rim and braided cord netting in 1893. The basket bottom was fitted with a chain which the referee pulled after a goal was scored and the ball rolled out. Surprisingly, it wasn't until 1912 that the open-bottomed net was approved for official play.

One aspect of the game that seems indispensable today came about as a matter of necessity. Young boys would sit on the balcony of Naismith's gym during games, their legs dangling through the banisters, and kick the ball away from the basket. To thwart the young kickers, a wooden rectangular shield—a backboard—for each basket was devised.

The early rules also made no provision for mounting the backboards out from the walls. In many gyms, backboards were simply hung on the walls like framed pictures. When driving in for a lay-up, a player had to be careful not to smash into the wall. Some players learned to climb the wall as

Made in accordance with the latest league regulations.

Per pair, **$4.00**

Our Official Basket Ball is made in regulation size and shape, the cover of finest selected pebble grained leather. It is made in eight sections, with capless ends, and the workmanship throughout of highest quality. The bladder is made extra heavy and of purest red Para rubber. Each packed, complete, in box, and guaranteed perfect in every detail.

No. **M.** Official Basket Ball, Each, **$6.00**

No. **16.** Basket Ball, regulation size, fine leather cover, with capped ends and bladder of selected quality. Each ball, complete in box, **$3.00**

Our Complete Catalogue, Handsomely Illustrated, Mailed Free to Any Address.

A. G. SPALDING & BROS.,
NEW YORK.   CHICAGO.   PHILADELPHIA.

By 1896, when this advertisement appeared, "basket ball" had a ball of its own. Basket was the pull-chain type.

they drove in, which made the lay-up a cinch. The present-day rule stating that the backboard must be mounted outward from the wall goes back to 1916.

As the game developed and became more competitive, one rule proved troublesome. It stated that the first man touching a ball after it went out of bounds could throw the ball back into play. This led to wild free-for-alls every time the ball went out of bounds. Not until 1913 were the rules amended to state that when a man knocked a ball out of bounds, or was the last to touch it, a member of the *other* team should throw it back in.

Professional basketball followed on the heels of Dr. Naismith's invention by only a few years, the first pro league beginning play in 1898. The term "cagers," occasionally used in referring to basketball players today, dates to the game's early days. Some teams used taut netting or chicken wire around the court, giving the appearance that the game was being played inside a huge cage.

"Players would be thrown against the wire, and most of us would get cut several times," Barney Sedran, a 5-foot-4 forward for several early pro teams, once recalled. "The court was covered with blood. It was more like ice hockey than basketball."

It wasn't only the chicken wire that caused Sedran to bleed. The only fouls called were tripping, hacking, and punching. Charging, holding, and pushing were ignored.

Some early professional games were played on caged-in courts like this one, which was erected in 1919 in a Paterson, New Jersey, armory.

The Original Celtics in 1923, (left to right) Johnny Beckman, Johnny Whitty, Nat Holman, John Barry, and Chris Leonard.

In one three-game series, Sedran received a two-stitch cut over the right eye on the first night, a similar wound over the other eye in the second game, and a second two-stitch cut over the right eye on the third night.

"I kept playing," he says. "You couldn't leave the game in those days, because once you were out, you weren't allowed back in." By the late 1920s, most basketball "cages" had been torn down.

During the pro game's first decades, teams and leagues came and went with the frequency of winter snowstorms. One exception was a team known as the Original Celtics. Started in 1914 in New York as a semipro team, the Celtics went on to dominate the American Basketball League, which was formed in 1925. One season—1927–28—the Celtics won 109 of 120 games. They were ruled out of the league the following season for being "too strong." Their star players earned as much as $10,000 a year, big money in those days, and the team barnstormed throughout the East, South, and Midwest.

Joe Lapchick, the 6-foot-5 son of a Yonkers, New York, policeman, joined the Celtics in 1923, as the team's starting center. He once described what the pro game was like in those days: "You carried your own uniform from game to game, night after night, with or without sleep, and with no relief for aches and pains. The team had no time for alibis, excuses, or explanations. If you complained about anything, you were gutless.

"I believe the Celtics were twenty years ahead of their time. They introduced switching on defense, the give-and-go, and the pivot play. They were the first team to operate as a unit, with none of the members playing for other teams." The Celtics kept right on going through the 1930s, and made their final appearance in an exhibition game against a team composed of members of the New York Giants football squad at Madison Square Garden in 1941.

Basketball as a college sport developed on a regional basis, with teams in the East displaying a style much different from those in the Midwest or on the Pacific Coast. Not until the mid-1930s,

Joe Lapchick was one of pro basketball's first "name" players.

17

when Madison Square Garden in New York began to promote college doubleheaders, drawing teams from all parts of the country, did college basketball take on national importance.

Professional basketball assumed a major-league look in the years that followed World War II. On June 6, 1946, an organizational meeting was held in New York City out of which came the Basketball Association of America. Those attending the meeting included such people as Walter Brown, president of the Boston Garden, lawyer Arthur Morse, who represented the owners of the Chicago Stadium, and Ned Irish, well known for his association with Madison Square Garden. They were all members of the Arena Managers Association, and their chief motive in organizing a basketball league was to provide entertainment for local fans on nights their stadiums ·were not occupied by their hockey teams.

They patterned their new league after the National Hockey League which had been founded twenty-nine years before. It is no coincidence that pro basketball is similar to pro hockey in many respects. Both sports have the same playoff systems. The financial policies of pro basketball resemble hockey's in that the home team keeps 100 percent of the gate receipts. In baseball and pro football, the visiting team shares in what comes through the ticket windows. Even basketball's annual guide is much the same as hockey's in style and format.

The first BAA basketball game was played in a venerable hockey arena, Maple Leaf Gardens in Toronto, on November 1, 1946. About 8,000 fans attended. The New York Knicks defeated the Toronto Huskies, 68–66.

The BAA was not the only league operating at the time. Indeed, the BAA didn't even have the best players. They belonged to the National Basketball League, which had been founded in 1937. The NBL, while it operated in some major cities—Chicago, Detroit, and Indianapolis—was also saddled with franchises in such whistle-stops as Sheboygan, Wisconsin, and Anderson, Indiana. Before the season of 1948-49 got under way, several NBL franchises were absorbed by the BAA. The following season the BAA changed its name to the National Basketball Association.

Flip through the pages of the *NBA Official Guide* and look at the photographs of the championship teams of the late 1940s and early 1950s, and you may notice one glaring difference from today's teams; they were all white. Pro basketball, in its early years, was exclusively a white man's game.

There were countless talented black players on independent teams, both professional and amateur. There were the barnstorming Harlem Globetrotters, who played before capacity crowds night after night.

Branch Rickey had sent shock waves through the world of sports when he signed infielder Jackie Robinson to a Brooklyn Dodger contract in 1946.

But the teams that made up the fledging Basketball Association of America saw no necessity of following Rickey's lead.

Not until the league's college draft in 1950 were blacks finally admitted to the NBA. That year Walter Brown, who held the Boston franchise, drafted Chuck Cooper, a 6-foot-6 All-American from Duquesne. In a later round, Mike Uline of the Washington Capitols picked Earl Lloyd of West Virginia State.

During the 1960s, blacks came to dominate the sport. Two-thirds of the players in the NBA today are black. When the Golden State Warriors won the NBA championship in 1974–75, they did it with a coaching staff and playing roster that had only one white man—Rick Barry. In the years from 1955 through 1976, the NBA's most valuable player award went to blacks 17 times. The NBA was the first pro league to have a black coach in Bill Russell of the Seattle SuperSonics and, before that, the Boston Celtics, and a black general manager in Wayne Embry of the Milwaukee Bucks.

The reason for black dominance is easy to perceive: basketball is the game of the urban poor. You don't need expensive equipment to play the game, merely a hoop and a ball. You don't need much space, only a rectangle of asphalt or concrete.

But the impact that blacks have had upon pro basketball is not expressed merely in terms of numbers of players and management personnel. It is also reflected in the way the game is played. There is a "black" style of play; there is also a "white" style. These differences, it must be stressed, developed for environmental reasons, not genetic ones. Or, to put it another way, Harlem basketball is much different than the type of game played in a Newport, Kentucky, backyard.

Black basketball is typified by speed, quickness, and jumping ability. When Dave Cowens, the Celtics' center, well known for his leaping agility, was being scouted while attending Florida State University, he was often described as "a white kid who can really jump." If Cowens had been black, his skill might not have been so noteworthy.

Black basketball is also a game of dazzle, of "moves," of self-expression. David Wolf, in his book, *Foul!*, explains why this may be true: "For many young men in the slums, the schoolyard is the only place they can feel true pride in what they do, where they can move free of inhibitions and where they can, by being spectacular, rise for the moment against the drabness and anonymity of their lives." A slam-dunk or a reverse lay-up gives a boy individuality, makes him special.

This topic was carefully examined by Jeff Greenfield in an article in *Esquire* magazine. Greenfield described white basketball as being common to Midwest gyms, Southern dirt courts, and black-topped and concrete suburban driveways. White basketball is a game of patience, method, and pre-

Television helped basketball win millions of new fans. Here regional basketball telecasts are coordinated at CBS' command center in New York.

cision. For years, the Boston Celtics played white basketball, running the fast break until the opposition was ready to drop. There was little that was creative about it. Everyone careened down the court. The ball would go to John Havlicek, who would pull up and pop a jumper or fake the shot and pass off to a teammate.

One reason that pro basketball delayed integrating was because some owners believed that white fans would be reluctant to pay to watch black players. There is no evidence that this ever happened. Fans proved color blind. The game showed consistent growth in most areas during the 1950s.

Basketball was televised for the first time in 1940 when station W2XBS in New York transmitted a college game, Fordham vs. Pittsburgh, from Madison Square Garden. Eventually, network television would help to win millions of fans for the sport.

The National Basketball Association became truly national in 1960 when the Minneapolis Lakers moved to Los Angeles. There were eight teams in operation that season. By the beginning of the next decade, the league had expanded to 17 teams.

In 1967 the NBA was challenged by a new league, the American Basketball Association. "They'll never finish the season," said some observers. The ABA did finish the season; the league finished nine of them, in fact.

Two innovations won the league a good amount of newspaper space. One was the three-point goal, awarded on any basket from beyond 25 feet, and which worked to increase the entertainment value of games.

The other innovation was the red, white, and blue basketball. Players liked it because for the first time they could see what type of spin and how much of it they were putting on their shots.

The ABA developed some outstanding players. These included a number of quick and mobile forwards, players such as Julius Erving and David Thompson, and formidable centers, Artis Gilmore and Len Elmore, to name two.

Speed and finesse were what you saw when you watched an ABA contest. The league was not as physical as the NBA, nor was there as much emphasis on defense.

David Thompson of the Denver Nuggets

There didn't seem to be as much emphasis on making money, either. Shaky franchises abounded, with some clubs hopscotching from one city to the next, hardly pausing to play games. Players were dealt and redealt at a dizzying rate. In many parts of the country, newspapers did not carry ABA results or standings, and the league never achieved much national television exposure. Merger talks were held as early as 1970.

When the agreement between the two leagues was finally hammered out, four ABA teams were taken into the NBA—the New York Nets, the San Antonio Spurs, the Denver Nuggets, and the Indiana Pacers. Three teams—the Virginia Squires, Spirits of St. Louis, and Kentucky Colonels—were permitted to expire, and their players were parceled out to NBA clubs.

After the merger, the NBA looked like this:

WESTERN CONFERENCE

Pacific Division

Golden State Warriors
Los Angeles Lakers
Phoenix Suns
Portland Trail Blazers
Seattle SuperSonics

Midwest Division

Chicago Bulls
Denver Nuggets
Detroit Pistons
Indiana Pacers
Kansas City Kings
Milwaukee Bucks

In 1975-76, the ABA's final season of existence, the league's teams were (left to right) the Virginia Squires, Spirits of St. Louis, Kentucky Colonels, San Diego Sails, Utah Stars, Indiana Pacers, San Antonio Spurs, New York Nets, and Denver Nuggets. Pacers, Spurs, Nets, and Nuggets were taken into the NBA.

EASTERN CONFERENCE

Central Division	Atlantic Division
Atlanta Hawks	Boston Celtics
Cleveland Cavaliers	Buffalo Braves
Houston Rockets	New York Knickerbockers
New Orleans Jazz	New York Nets
San Antonio Spurs	Philadelphia 76ers
Washington Bullets	

A new playoff system was introduced which permitted twelve teams to qualify. Each of the four division champions automatically gain a playoff berth. The other eight spots are filled by the four teams with the best records in the Eastern and Western Conferences.

The playoffs are sometimes called the "second season," an appropriate term. The word "season" is especially good, for playoff competition goes on for weeks and weeks. In one recent year, for example, the playoffs began in mid-April with the conference qualifying rounds. Then came the conference semifinals, the conference finals, and, ultimately, the championship series. The baseball season was deep into its second month of play and the calendar read June 7 before the title was finally decided.

It is not likely that James Naismith, who, after all, thought up basketball as a wintertime diversion, would have approved. There were other changes in the sport that also displeased him.

After joining the faculty of the University of Kansas in 1898 as director of physical education, he introduced basketball to the campus and coached the varsity team for a while. When the rules were revised so as to require the team on offense to get the ball over the midcourt line in ten seconds, Naismith remarked, "From a pastime played all over the court, and which required a good degree of smart maneuvering, basketball now has evolved into one of speed, confusion, and congestion, because all the ball handling and passing has to be done in one-half the court."

Later, when the center jump after each field goal

was eliminated, Naismith disapproved again. "Some of the game's cleverest and most thrilling plays came on premeditated moves around the center jump," he said.

Dr. Naismith stayed at the University of Kansas for more than forty years. He died in 1939 at the age of seventy-eight.

He never made much money from the sport. The average professional player's salary today is over $100,000, and superstars are millionaires. But the inventor of the game earned only $3,000 a year as a professor in the Department of Physical Education at Kansas, and during the Great Depression he stood by helplessly as his home was seized by a loan company.

Naismith has been well remembered, however. The Naismith Memorial Hall of Fame, opened in Springfield, Massachusetts, in 1968, does him honor. But more than that, as Bernice Larson Webb, his biographer, has noted, "Every rusted basketball hoop fastened ten feet high on a pole, tree, garage, or barn wherever children gather to play . . . is a memorial to the man and a tribute to the game of basketball."

EQUIPMENT, RULES, STATISTICS

Basketball equipment is much the same today as it was in the winter of 1891, when James Naismith invented the game. All you needed then was a round ball, a hoop, and a level place to play, and that's about all you need today.

The ball has been changed a trifle. The first teams continued to use soccer balls to play "basket ball" until 1894, the year a maker of bicycles in Chicopee, Massachusetts—the Overman Wheel Company—began to manufacture and sell the first basketballs. Before the century ended, the A. G. Spalding Company replaced the Overman firm as the manufacturer of the game's official ball. Other manufacturers entered the field during the early 1900s, including Wilson, Rawlings, and Voit.

The size of the ball changed several times, and it was once as large as 32 inches in circumference. The ball used today cannot be any more than 30 inches in circumference nor less than 29½ inches. It has to weigh between 20 and 22 ounces. Before each game, the referee checks the three balls to be used in the game to see that air pressure of each is between 7½ and 8½ pounds.

The American Basketball Association, as mentioned in the previous section, introduced a red, white, and blue ball when the league set up shop in 1967. But color wasn't its only unique feature. It also had a smoother surface than the NBA ball.

The official ball—7½-8½ pounds of air pressure, 29½ to 30 inches in circumference.

Players who switched from the ABA to the NBA found the NBA ball easier to handle with sweaty hands.

A player today wouldn't think of stepping out on the court without sneakers on his feet, but sneakers were unknown until 1903, the year that the Spalding Company advertised the first "suction sole" shoes. Today, of course, sneakers are available in a wide array of styles. And no wonder. During the course of a game, a pro player may run seven or eight miles, and he's constantly starting and stopping and changing direction. The feet take a terrific pounding. Sneakers are a way of pampering them.

Pro players wear two pairs of socks to cut·down on the chafing of the feet inside the sneakers. The socks are usually 50 percent wool and 50 percent synthetic fiber. They're always white, with the outer fails to have the taping done.

Low-cut sneakers are in vogue today. Players feel that they're more light-footed when they wear

Sneaker styles cover a wide range. Some players go through two dozen pairs in a season.

low cuts as opposed to the old high cuts, which covered the ankle. As far as supporting the ankle is concerned, there's no evidence that high-cuts were in any way beneficial in this regard. Besides, all pro players have their ankles taped before a game and practice sessions. Some teams fine any player who fails to have the taping done.

Players want their sneakers to fit as snugly as possible. Often they're from one-half a size to one full size smaller than their street shoes. Again, the reason is to prevent chafing. Of course, no one wants a sneaker so tight that it's going to cramp one's foot or, worse, cut off circulation.

Players wear out sneakers at a rapid clip. George McGinnis of the 76ers goes through about two dozen pairs of his size 14½ sneakers each season, sometimes bursting the seams with his sharp cuts and quick stops.

While the game's equipment has changed little over the years, basketball rules have been subject to considerable revision. Naismith's first rules specified that the basket was to be 10 feet above the floor. That's one of the few rules that hasn't been changed at all.

The court today is wider and longer than the one laid out by Naismith. The diagram here gives modern court dimensions for pro basketball.

While the court has become bigger, the amount of playing time has diminished. A game used to be

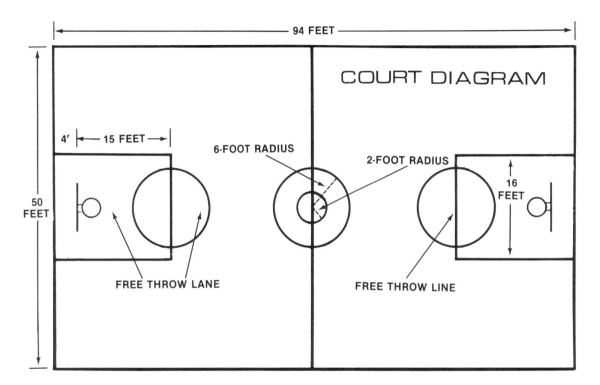

94 FEET

COURT DIAGRAM

4′ ← 15 FEET →

6-FOOT RADIUS

2-FOOT RADIUS

50 FEET

16 FEET

FREE THROW LANE

FREE THROW LINE

60 minutes long. A pro game today is 48 minutes in length, divided into 12-minute quarters. There's a time-out period of 15 minutes at the half, and 90-second time-out periods between the first and second quarters, and the third and fourth quarters.

All overtime periods are five minutes in length. As many overtime periods are played as are necessary to determine a winner.

Each team is granted seven timeouts during a game, each of which is 90 seconds in length. No more than four timeouts are permitted in the fourth period. Any player on the floor is eligible to call a timeout, but it's rare for a player to call one without it first being called by his coach.

One other rule specifies that there must be at least two timeouts every period. In the event neither coach calls a timeout, the official scorer calls time. The first timeout, according to the rules, must be

"Timeout!" calls Paul Silas.

taken before the sixth minute of play is completed, and charged to the home team. The second timeout is called before the ninth minute, and is charged to the visiting team.

Radio and television are the reason for this rule. The timeouts give sponsors an opportunity to promote their products.

Making a field goal was the only way a team could score in basketball's earliest days; there were no free throws. A field goal was worth only one point.

While infractions of the rules were called "fouls," the method of punishment resembled the system used in ice hockey. When a player was guilty of two consecutive fouls—pushing, tripping, or holding—he was removed from the game, and the team played one man short until either side scored a goal. Then the man was permitted to return.

A second foul rule stated that when players on a team were guilty of three fouls without the other team committing any, the offended team was to be awarded one point.

The concept of penalizing a team by permitting the offended team an unopposed chance to score—a "free" throw—dates to 1894. Since a field goal and free throw were equal in value at the time, the free throw was deemed a heavy penalty for the offending team to bear. The solution was to adjust the scoring system, to make a field goal worth two points and a free throw worth only half as much.

This system worked so well that it has remained in effect to this day.

When the American Basketball Association set up shop in 1967, it revised the scoring system, adopting a three-point basket (in addition to the two-point field goal and one-point free throw). An arc was drawn on the floor 25 feet from the hoop (see diagram). Any shot into the basket from beyond the line was counted as three points.

ABA players made approximately 30 percent of all shots attempted from beyond 25 feet, and some

ABA games featured a three-point field goal for any basket shot from beyond 25 feet (shaded area).

players became exceptionally skilled in hitting them. In a game against San Antonio in 1974, Billy Keller of the Indiana Pacers netted nine three-point goals, the one-game record for three-pointers at the time the ABA folded in 1975.

Basketball's free-throw distance was 20 feet at first, then later reduced to the present distance— 15 feet. Each team was permitted a specialist to do the foul shooting, much as today's pro football teams have place-kicking and punting specialists. Specialization in basketball ended in 1924.

The foul rules soon proved less than perfect and many abuses developed. Players learned to foul on purpose. When a player on Team A was driving in for a basket, a player on Team B might clobber him. The penalty was one free throw. Even if the fouled player made the shot, Team B was still ahead of the game, for they had prevented the man from scoring a field goal. In addition, Team B, following the free throw, had an opportunity to gain possession of the ball.

So the penalty for fouling was made harsher. A rule was introduced that provided for "fouling out." It stated that a player who committed a second foul was disqualified, although a substitute player could be sent in to replace him. The limit in fouls was later increased from two to five, reduced to four for a time, and then set at five once more. In the modern pro game, the limit is six.

Other rule infractions were not termed fouls but

were "violations." Running with the ball, double dribbling, stepping over a boundary line while putting the ball in play were included in this category. The penalty was to give the ball over to the other team.

Trial and error development of the rules continued through the years. But as late as the 1950s, there were obvious deficiencies in the game. A team would frequently stall once it had built a decisive lead, and stalling is never exciting to watch. Deliberate fouling was still common.

Professional basketball overcame these shortcomings in 1954 with two rules that did much to improve the game. One was the 24-second rule. It stated that a team had to shoot at the basket, and at least hit the rim or the backboard, within 24 seconds after getting possession. If the team failed to shoot within 24 seconds, it was a violation and the other team was handed possession of the ball out of bounds. Timers that could easily be seen by the players were placed at each corner of the court.

The idea for the 24-second rule was advanced by Danny Biasone, owner of the Syracuse Nationals. But many owners opposed the idea. Milton Gross, a columnist for the *New York Post*, summed up their feelings when he wrote that "ball handling now becomes a liability" and he lamented the loss of the "strategic freeze."

But the benefits of the new rule far outweighed any failings it might have had. The 24-second timer

The 24-second timer did much to improve the quality of pro games.

ended stalling. Or at least a team couldn't stall for any more than 23 seconds.

And the blinking clocks had a striking effect on scoring. During the season of 1953–54, only one player, Neil Johnston of the Philadelphia Warriors, was able to average as many as 20 points a game. In the first season that the timer was in use, four players topped 20 points, and two years later, eight players exceeded that figure. Team scoring averages also dramatically increased. The Celtics averaged 101.4

points per game during the first season that the timer was in use. Only one team, also the Celtics, had averaged as many as 85 points the previous season.

The second new rule made the penalty for fouling stiffer, introducing the concept of the "team foul." This rule now states that a team can commit four personal fouls in a quarter without penalty. But after that, the offended team gets an extra free throw. In what would normally be a one free-throw foul situation, the offended team gets two shots. In a two free-throw foul situation, the team gets three shots.

Two other aspects of the rules governing fouls must be mentioned. One has to do with offensive fouls. An offensive foul is one committed by a member of the team that has possession of the ball. Charging is a typical offensive foul.

It used to be that when the offensive team was guilty of a foul, the other team got one penalty shot. The offensive team then got the ball back. Since the penalty was mild and the offending team did not lose possession, deliberate offensive fouls were not uncommon.

But now the rules state that when a team commits an offensive foul, the ball is handed over to the defensive team, that is, the team takes the ball out of bounds. There is no free throw. A personal foul is charged to the player who committed the foul, but it is not counted as a team foul.

The penalty is the same in the case of what is

Flags like these are used to notify officials of total fouls incurred. "P1" means "first personal foul"; "T1" means "first team foul," etc.

called a "loose ball foul," a foul that is committed by a player in pursuit of a free ball or a rebound. It is termed a "loose" ball because neither team has clear-cut possession of it. In such cases, there is no free throw; the ball is simply given to the offended team.

Several infractions are penalized by awarding the offended team two free throws. This is the penalty assessed when a man is fouled in the act of shooting for the basket, or when a man is breaking for the basket, is past all defenders, and is fouled from behind.

Two foul shots are also awarded in the case of a "backcourt foul." A backcourt foul is one committed by the defending team while the offense is in control of the ball within that half of the floor containing the basket it is defending. Finally, any foul committed while the ball is out of bounds results in a two-shot penalty.

All of the above are personal fouls, so-called be-

Bill Bradley risks a techni-cal foul.

cause they involve contact, one player interfering with the play of an opponent. But there are also technical fouls, those that do not involve contact. A technical foul can be assessed, not only against a player, but against a coach, an assistant coach, or any other nonplaying member of the team who is on the bench.

A technical foul can be called for unsportsmanlike conduct on the part of a player or coach, for the verbal abuse of an official or the use of profanity, for delaying a game by preventing the ball from being put in play, or requesting and being charged with an extra timeout. A technical foul calls for one free throw. The team in possession of the ball before the calling of the foul is given the ball again.

The paragraphs above explain the game's most important rules. The rules in their entirety are to be found in the *NBA Official Guide*, which is available from *The Sporting News* (1212 North Lindbergh Boulevard, St. Louis, Missouri 63166). It costs $3. The book, which is more than 400 pages in length, also contains team directories, player rosters, records, and statistics.

It takes dozens of people to stage a professional game. The referees are probably the most important of these. There are two referees assigned to each game. One usually stations himself near the offensive team's basket, the other near the midcourt line, and

Whistle at the ready, referee Norm Drucker studies game action.

they move with the flow of play.

It is generally acknowledged that pro referees are not quite as strict in their enforcement of the rules as their college counterparts. "In the pros we try to decide whether a man gains an advantage by doing certain things," one referee says. "If he walks and doesn't gain any advantage by it, we might not call it. We allow a man to put his hands on an opponent, and as long as he doesn't hamper his free movement by holding, it's just 'loving' him as far as we're concerned."

Despite their tendency toward leniency, pro referees are the most criticized of all sports officials. In baseball and football, the fans are well removed from the field of play. But in basketball they're much closer. When a referee sounds his whistle and prepares to announce an infraction, the fans get ready to make *their* judgment. Boos and catcalls are often the result.

It's not only the fans who misbehave. The coaches often heap abuse upon the referees and so do the players. A professional football player might say a few words of criticism to an official, and baseball players can be outspoken, but basketball players express themselves more often and more heatedly than athletes in any other professional sport. When a player uses profanity or makes physical contact

As players charge down court, so does Drucker.

After spotting violation, Drucker signals the scorer's table.

with a referee, a technical foul quickly follows. But the resulting penalty, one foul shot for the opposition, is not considered much of a deterrent.

One problem for officials is the growing number of "actors," that is, players who pretend to be fouled in order to be awarded a free throw. Kevin Porter used to step in front of an opposition player and fall to the floor, hoping to draw a charging foul. He had a high percentage of success. Phil Chenier of the Bullets is said to be another expert in the art.

It's usual for a small man to try to victimize a bigger, more aggressive man. Dave Cowens of the Celtics is, thus, a frequent victim. Cowens says that not only is the number of smaller pretenders on the rise, but that the big defensive players are taking to falling down, too. He's afraid that the practice is going to become an accepted piece of strategy.

To be selected as a referee in the NBA, it's recommended that a candidate be a member of the International Association of Basketball Officials, a nonprofit group dedicated to the advancement of basketball officiating. To gain membership, you must pass a written examination and a "floor" test, in which game action is simulated.

The NBA maintains working agreements with several independent leagues, including the Southern California Summer Professional League, the Eastern Basketball Association, and the Rucker League, in which prospective officials receive on-the-job training. Whether it is by this method or some other, it's vital that candidates get experience in "blowing the

The official clock is controlled by this console.

whistle," says John Nucatola, the NBA's Supervisor of Officials.

The game officials are assisted by two timers. One of them operates the 24-second clock, the other the game clock. There's also an official scorer. He keeps track of field goals, free throws, team and individual fouls, and timeouts. It's the scorer who notifies the referee when a sixth personal foul has been called upon players.

Like every other professional sport, basketball produces a great outpouring of statistical information. In every game, statistics for the below-named categories are compiled for each player and listed in the game's box score:

1. Minutes played (Min.)
2. Field goals made (FGM)
3. Field goals attempted (FGA)

4. Free throws made (FTM)
5. Free throws attempted (FTA)
6. Rebounds (Reb.)
    Offensive (Off.)
    Defensive (Def.)
    Total (Tot.)
7. Assists (Ast.)
8. Personal Fouls (PF)
9. Disqualified (Disq.)
10. Steals (Stls.)
11. Points (Pts.)

In addition, shooting percentages are figured for field goals and free throws, and totals are listed for rebounds and technical fouls. Losing the ball to the opposition without getting at least one try for the basket is called a turnover, and the official box-score of a game now includes the total number of turnovers for each team.

Score sheet used in compiling game's statistics.

While the statistics have some value in comparing one player's performance with another's, they can be deceiving. Statistics only tell you how much; they never say how or when.

Take field goals as an example. Let's suppose that Player A makes 3 of 12 field goals, a .250 percentage, and Player B makes 5 of 10 field goals, a .500 percentage. Which player had the better game? You really can't say. Player B's field goals may have been the result of lay-ups and tap-ins, while Player A's may have been shot from 20 or 25 feet. And Player A may have scored under pressure, perhaps toward the end of the game when the score was close and points sorely needed. Player B's points may have been scored routinely.

The totals for rebounds can also lead one to the wrong conclusions. Player A may have 6 rebounds for a game; Player B has 4. But those rebounds credited to Player B may have been ones that he had to fight for, while Player A's rebounds may have come as a result of favorable caroms off the rim or backboard. He just happened to be in the right place at the right time.

It's also true that sometimes information presented in the box score is colored by hometown favoritism. The official scorers and statisticians are hired by the home teams. It's only natural that they favor hometown players, however unprofessional that may be.

The most telling evidence as to scorers' partiality concerns the statistics for assists. An assist is a pass that leads to a field goal. The problem is that scorers differ as to when a pass is an assist pass and when it is not. In one recent season, Kevin Porter of the Washington Bullets had back-to-back games of 21 and 22 assists at the very end of the schedule to run away with the assists title for the year. Both games were played at home. To have 15 assists in a game is excellent. To have 21 in one game and 22 the next is exceptional—or questionable. *Sports Illustrated* reported that Porter was once credited with two assists in 41 seconds, but later it was discovered that the Bullets did not score a point during that span.

Statistical totals for rebounds is another category that can be affected by the scorer's judgment. The rebound leader for the 1974–75 season was Wes Unseld of the Bullets. He had an average of 14.8 rebounds for each game, beating out Dave Cowens who averaged 14.7 per game. But Unseld managed to win the title in his final regular season game with a 30-rebound performance. The game was played on Washington's home court.

"It's ridiculous," said Red Auerbach, general manager of Cowens' team, the Celtics. "Every time a guy touches the ball they give him a rebound. Assists? They don't mean the same thing in any two cities in the league."

Actually, players such as Dave Cowens are habitually short-changed by statistics, whether or not they are victimized by scorers' favoritism. Cowens is an aggressive rebounder and a potent

Foot injury kept Nets' Nate (Tiny) Archibald on the sidelines through much of 1976-77 season.

scorer. He blocks shots and scrambles on the floor for loose balls. He would just as soon pass off as shoot. But because he is so versatile, he has never led the league in any one statistical category. All he has done is help his team win the NBA championship a couple of times.

Steals and blocked shots are other categories in which the scorer's subjectivity may be reflected.

But it isn't merely the possible partisanship of the official scorer that should cause you to look upon statistics with some skepticism. After all, the scorer, no matter how much of a "homer," can't affect such categories as field goals and free throws made, fouls, minutes played, and some others. No, it is the numbers themselves. While accurate, they can mislead you.

When you attend a game, don't make the mistake that many fans do and watch only the ball and where it goes. By doing so, you may miss some of the game's most dramatic features.

The more you know about each team in advance, the greater your enjoyment is going to be. From the local newspaper, you can learn what injuries a team may have, and who the substitute players are going to be. Not only injuries, but fatigue can affect a team, too. Ask yourself where the visiting team played the night before. For example, a team that is in Los Angeles to face the Lakers is not going to be up to par if it happened to arrive in the city at 5:00 A.M. on a flight from Milwaukee following a difficult game.

Match-up: Lucius Allen of the Lakers vs. Bullets' Phil Chenier.

Know the playing style of each of the starters. What is each man's favorite shot? What is his favorite shooting location? Elvin Hayes, for example, leaps about as high as any player in the game, and falls back when he shoots. How does the opposition center cope with Hayes' shot? Marvin Barnes delivers a strange-looking shot, starting it from somewhere behind his head. How does anyone defend against *that*? When George McGinnis posts inside, he is almost sure to go to the basket. What does the opposition do to try to stop McGinnis?

In other words, you should become aware of the match-ups, the individual offensive-defensive struggles between opposing players. Is the offensive man able to play his game, or is the defensive man who is covering him forcing him to do something different?

An interesting match-up took place during the final NBA playoff series in 1976, the Boston Celtics vs. the Phoenix Suns. The Celts had hustling, aggressive Dave Cowens at center. The Suns' center was slight and stylish Alvan Adams, then in his rookie season. In the first two games, Cowens was able to be his intimidating self, dominating the boards and shooting passes to Jo Jo White, who would either score himself or set up a teammate. All in all, Cowens and his teammates were able to push the Suns around. The Celtics won the two games with ease.

But when the series moved to Phoenix, the presence of hometown fans stirred Adams and his teammates. Adams was the principal reason Cowens fouled out of the third game, and he also scored 33 points and had 14 rebounds, and the Suns won.

Ultimately, the series came down to the seventh game. Once more Cowens prevailed over Adams.

NO.	NAME	POINTS	TOT.	P.F.
15	Dudley	2 4 ⑤ ⑥ /9 ⑩ 12 14 //16	16	1/1/2/34
41	Wilkes	2 ③ 5 7/9 11 ⑫ /16 18/20 22	22	12/3/4/

With the score 68-67, Boston, Cowens, carrying the burden of five fouls, stole Adams' dribble, then barreled down the court and was fouled by Adams as he went up for the shot. At another critical point not long before the game's end, Cowens beat Adams on a spin move to the basket. There were many other factors involved, of course, but the Celtics won the NBA championship that year more because Cowens was able to play his game than for any other reason.

You should also know the basic offensive strategy of each of the opposing teams. Some teams like to fast-break; others prefer to be more deliberate, using set plays. If you're a fan of the Boston Celtics, you should keep aware of how well your team is rebounding, for unless a fast-breaking team can command the boards, they're not going to be successful.

Always try to tell whether the players on your team are working together. Is there plenty of movement? No one should ever be standing still.

You can also enhance your enjoyment of a game by keeping your own statistics. All you need is a large sheet of ruled paper. Divide it in half with a heavy line down the middle of the page. One half of the page is devoted to one team's scoring, the other half to the other team.

Rule each side into five columns. The widest column is to be used to record each player's cumulative point total during the game. Smaller spaces are for each man's name and the personal fouls each

incurs. Still smaller spaces are for each player's number and point total.

Whenever a player scores a field goal, simply add two points to his cumulative total. When he scores a free throw, add one point to the total. Put a circle around each free-throw entry. This will help you to distinguish free throws from field goals at any time during the game.

When a quarter ends, enter a vertical line just to the right of each player's total. This will enable you to determine each man's scoring total for each quarter. If a player does not play, or plays but does not score during a quarter, the two vertical lines you draw will appear adjacent to one another (as shown in the line devoted to Dudley in the illustrated example).

Keep track of personal fouls in the same fashion, entering the cumulative total for each player. Again, use vertical lines to indicate the quarter.

You can also keep track of assists, rebounds, and shots taken. But don't be surprised if the figures that you compile for these categories do not agree with those that appear in the newspaper account of the game the next day. It's the official scorer who decides when a player should be credited with assists and rebounds, and you can't except to be in agreement with him in every case.

Hank Luisetti

THE SKILLS

It was a mild December night in 1936. Two weeks before, the Green Bay Packers had beaten the Boston Redskins for the pro football championship. Sonja Henie was starring in "One in a Million" at the Roxy Theatre in New York. Louisiana State University was favored over Santa Clara in the Sugar Bowl.

At Madison Square Garden, basketball was on the program. Stanford University faced Long Island University. Every seat was filled.

No one gave the Stanford team much of a chance. The LIU Blackbirds, winners of 43 consecutive games, ranked as one of the nation's most powerful teams. When the Blackbirds scored first, their supporters settled back to watch the team add another victory to their long string.

But they were quickly jarred out of their complacency by a slender, dark-haired Stanford forward by the name of Angelo (Hank) Luisetti. Time after time, Luisetti would swoop down the court with a graceful stride and, without pausing, fire at the basket one-handed. The first time he did it the fans and opposing players could hardly believe their eyes. No one shot with one hand in those days, and no one shot on the run. Of course, you might use one hand on a lay-up or when taking a hook shot, but never from far out on the floor.

The two-handed set shot was what everyone relied upon. You planted your feet, gripped the ball in both hands at about your chin, aimed by sighting over the top of it, then thrust it toward the basket.

Not only did Luisetti startle the huge crowd by shooting one-handed, his shots went in. With Luisetti scoring Stanford's first five field goals, the West Coast team surged to an 8-point lead at half-time.

LIU managed to reduce the Stanford lead to 6 points soon after the final period began. Then Luisetti went to work again. In the space of less than two minutes, he arched in two one-handers and two foul shots. Then he passed to Howie Turner, the other Stanford forward, for another field goal, and started another play on which guard Jack Calderwood scored. It added up to 10 points. LIU never recovered.

The final score saw Stanford on top, 45-31. Luisetti, taken out of the game in the final minutes to receive a tremendous ovation, scored 15 points, a remarkably high total for the day.

"It seemed Luisetti could do nothing wrong," said *The New York Times* in its account of the game. "Some of his shots would have been deemed foolish if attempted by anyone else, but with Luisetti shooting, they were accepted by the enchanted crowd."

Some of the local coaches who watched Luisetti's performance were not at all enchanted. "That's not basketball," snorted Nat Holman, who coached the City College team. "If my boys ever shot one-handed, I'd quit coaching." Holman called Luisetti's one-hander "more of a prayer than a shot."

Holman saw more of Luisetti's prayerful play the next season, when Hank was a senior. Stanford came into New York to whip LIU by 15 points and City College by 3 points. In the second half of the game against City College, Luisetti scored 13 straight points. One newspaperman called it "a breathtaking exhibition of exquisite artistry."

Eventually, Nat Holman came to recognize Luisetti's talents. "Hank was an amazing marksman," he was to say years later. "He was also a spectacular dribbler and an astonishingly deft passer. He was one of the finest and most capable players I ever saw."

But few people remember Luisetti for his versatility. It was his one-hand shot that won him his fame, for it triggered a basketball revolution. After Luisetti's performance in Madison Square Garden that December night in 1936, youngsters everywhere started popping the ball with one hand. Coaches of the time eventually became convinced that the one-hander was a legitimate weapon.

The best evidence of the change that took place is what happened to the two-handed set shot. Like the hula hoop and touch dancing, it's almost extinct. If a player were to come down the court today, solidly plant both feet, and grasp the ball in both hands to shoot, he'd be laughed right off the court.

Butch Beard of the Knicks tries a running one-hander from amidst a covey of Celtics.

He also would probably have the ball stolen from him, with the stealer driving in to score.

Of course, you don't see running one-handers much either. Pro players went beyond the one-hand shot to the jump shot.

The first pro to display a successful jumper was Joe Fulks, a forward for the Philadelphia Warriors during the NBA's earliest days. Whether facing the basket or spinning around, Fulks would jump and with one hand pop the ball toward the basket at the top of his jump.

Fulks led the Warriors in the league championship in 1947, averaging 23.2 points per game. The next highest scorer that season was Bob Feerick of the Washington Capitols. Feerick, with a 16.3 average, was almost 7 points behind Fulks.

During the early 1950s, the jump shot became basektball's No. 1 offensive weapon. Such players as Paul Arizin, Bill Sharman, Ed Macauley, and Bob Pettit were among its leading practitioners. Today, of course, every player uses it. It's as basic to the game as hoops and backboards.

It is not difficult to understand why the jumper has become preeminent. It's the most reliable method there is to overcome a defender. If you veer to the right or left before you shoot, a defending player can move with you. But when you go straight up, perhaps first employing a feint or two, you're likely to leave the defensive man behind. The jumper also neutralizes the height advantage a taller defender has.

Paul Arizin, an early practitioner of jump shot.

Pacers' Billy Knight displays classic jumper.

Being up high not only gives you a good field of vision as far as the basket is concerned, it also enables you to see a breaking teammate. If you think there is someone else who has a better chance of making the shot, you can pass off at the last moment.

Another advantage of the jumper is one of stability. Almost all players pop the ball at the very top of their jump, during that split second that they have gone as high as they are going to go but have not yet started downward. They are hanging there motionless. It's almost as if their feet were firmly planted.

There are several ways of executing the jumper. Some players go straight up, while others lean forward or back. These last two methods have built-in advantages. When you lean toward the defender as you jump, you'll sometimes draw a foul. Lean back as you go up, and your shot, if accurate, will be just about as unstoppable as any shot can be. One reason that Wilt Chamberlain holds all those scoring records is because of the beautiful fall-away jumper he had.

Whether you lean forward or back, the idea is to shoot the ball off your fingertips. As you pump the ball toward the basket, your shooting arm becomes fully extended.

The jump shot is being used with even greater frequency nowadays. The sagging, helping defenses that teams are using have made driving to the

Charlie Dudley of the Warriors displays intruction-book form in executing a lay-up.

44

Pete Maravich drives in for a two-handed lay-up.

basket a risky business. Driving often results in a charging foul. Sometimes the only shot the offensive team can rely upon is the jump shot.

Of course, the lay-up, a bank shot taken near the backboard, is still a fundamental part of the game, and one of the surest methods of scoring. Skilled players make 90 percent of their lay-ups. The lay-up's drawback is that you need a clear path to the basket in order to execute it, and, as stated above, getting that clear path isn't quite as easy as it used to be.

The professional lay-up can be exotic, bearing little resemblance to the lay-up one sees in high school or college games. When Tiny Archibald drives in for a lay-up, he displays more moves than a jackrabbit. As he nears the basket and accelerates, he surges into the air, faking with his head, body, and feet. He's likely to switch the ball from one hand to the other and flip it up early, so as to avoid an opponent who is striving, not so much to block the shot, as to cause an offensive foul. Archibald has scored many hundreds of times on lay-ups, but it is safe to say that no two have been exactly alike.

Archibald also excels in executing a shot that is known as a "reverse lay-up." This is a lay-up that's put on from the far side of the basket after the player has actually passed beneath it.

It was mentioned above that pro players are successful on about 90 percent of their lay-ups. A shot that is even more reliable than the lay-up is the

Dan Issel of the Nuggets gets fancy with a reverse dunk.

"dunk" or "stuff." The player leaps in the air and slams the ball down through the hoop. It's seldom missed because you're shooting from above.

If a player is 7-feet tall, or almost that, and has long arms, it's no great feat to be able to dunk the ball, the basket being 10 feet from the floor. But there are countless pro players who are closer to 6 feet than they are to 7 feet who can leap high enough to stuff. Even Houston's Calvin Murphy, who stands 5-foot-9½, has a dunk shot.

Julius Erving of the Philadelphia 76ers has authored some of the most sensational dunk shots of all time. He takes to the air in a gravity-defying leap from a point somewhere near the foul line, drifts toward the hoop, and ends up slamming the ball down one-handed, two-handed, or with both hands bent back over his head. The crowd comes to its feet screaming.

Once Julius took part in a "Slam Dunk Contest" sponsored by a television network. After four other players had displayed their dunking skills, it was the Doctor's turn. In a remarkable tribute to him, the other players went out onto the floor to get closer and sat down. The master was about to perform. The Doctor won the contest.

The hook shot is another basic weapon. Usually it's executed from a pivot position, but occasionally players come into the league who can hook over long distances. Tommy Heinsohn, who played for and later coached the Boston Celtics, was one such player.

In executing the hook shot, you stand with your back to the basket, holding the ball in one hand away from your body. With your arm fully extended, you sweep the ball over your head toward the basket. Your body acts to block the defender.

If the player who is shooting the hook happens to be taller than the man who is defending him, his chances of blocking the shot are very slim. Dave Cowens, center for the Boston Celtics, increased the devastating quality of the hook shot by sometimes jumping as he uncorked one. In the early stages of his career, Cowens, who stood 6-foot-8½, was sometimes said to be too "short" to play center for a pro team. But no one who ever tried to defend against Cowens' jump hook ever made the statement.

In attempting hook shots, dunks, lay-ups, and jumpers, frontcourt players—centers and forwards—are supposed to be successful 50 percent of the time. The league average is about 46 percent.

Most shots from the floor are automatic in the way they're executed. Not the free throw, however. Like pitching a baseball or hitting a golf shot, with the free throw there's time to think.

For some players, this is a distinct disadvantage, especially in a tense situation. Wilt Chamberlain, the game's dominant player during the 1960s, is

Bullets' Wes Unseld tunes up his hook shot.

47

Rick Barry (here wearing All-Star uniform) is modern-day free-throw champion.

Left: Wilt Chamberlain—trouble at the foul line.

a case in point. Coaches want their players to hit 75 percent of their attempts from the foul line. Chamberlain never approached that figure. In the first four years of his career, he made close to 60 percent of his free throws, but then he began getting worse. In his fourteen years as a professional Wilt hit a mere 51 percent of his foul shots.

When Wilt played for the old Philadelphia Warriors, a private instructor named Sy Kaselman was hired to help him. A pro player of the 1920s, Kaselman had been successful on 247 of 261 free-throw attempts one season, earning an incredible 94.6 percentage. Kaselman could make foul shots one-handed, two-handed, standing with his back to the basket—that is, over his head—and blindfolded. But he could not help Chamberlain.

At one time or another during his career, Chamberlain tried every possible free-throw style—overhand and underhand, one hand and two hands. He tried shooting from several inches in back of the line. While Wilt got so he could make as many as 85 percent of his shots in practice sessions, he never approached that figure in games. His inability to make free throws dogged Wilt until the end of his career.

There are several techniques used in shooting fouls, with each player using the one that seems best for him. Rick Barry of the Golden State Warriors, with an .887 percentage, the No. 1 foul shooter of the mid-1970s, tossed the ball up underhand

49

Bill Sharman won fame for foul-shooting skill.

with two hands. One advantage of this method is that it enables the shooter to put favorable spin on the ball, so that if it hits the rim it is inclined to go in.

Despite Barry's success, the two-handed foul shooter remains a rarity. Most players use one hand, a style that was popularized by Bill Sharman, the most consistent foul shooter of all time. During the 1958-59 season, Sharman made 342 of the 367 free throws he attempted, giving him a .932 average, the best ever in pro basketball.

Sharman's Celtic teammates remember him as a perfectionist. "He was never satisfied," Frank Ramsey once recalled. "He was always competing within himself, always trying to be better. He'd make, say, 32 throws in a row and then miss one. Immediately he'd begin to analyze the one he missed, trying to figure out what he had done wrong. He was the fiercest competitor I ever met."

Gene Conley, another of his teammates, once told of an index card that Sharman always carried that listed things to remember during a game. "Every single night he read it," said Conley. "The card told him how to hold his hands on defense, how to release the ball when shooting, and how to position his feet at the foul line. He was still reading the card at the end of his career."

When Sharman took his stance at the foul line, he first took a deep breath to help him relax. Then he concentrated, wiping every distraction from his mind. His body would be loose, his knees slightly bent, his right foot pointed toward the basket, the left foot slightly back and at a 45-degree angle to the right.

He'd support the ball with both hands, sighting over it. He always aimed at the basket itself, never the backboard.

Before he took the shot, he'd waggle the ball to and fro a few times, so as to loosen his wrist and get the "feel" of the ball's weight. Then, with the ball resting on the tips of his fingers, he'd bend his wrist back, cocking it. The thrusting of the ball toward the basket would begin in the legs, move up through the body, and end with the straightening of the shooting arm. He kept his feet on the floor.

As the ball was released, it rolled off the fingers with a slight backspin. This helped the ball to "stick" to the rim when it hit it, instead of rebounding away.

Some players use a one-handed jumper at the foul line, actually leaving their feet as they release. Two-handed overhead shots are also seen. Whatever method is used, the "secret" to success is consistency, doing exactly the same thing on every shot, from the time you receive the ball from the referee until you put the shot away.

And you have to be relaxed as you shoot. As soon as a player has been fouled and has been awarded a shot, he'll begin preparing himself. The standard method for relaxing is to take four or five

Deep breathing helps George McGinnis relax at the foul line.

Caldwell Jones bounces the ball to reduce tension.

A pass has to be accurate and delivered at the right speed. Here Calvin Murphy tosses underhand.

the ball several times before shooting, then eye their target, really concentrate on it, and send the shot away.

The aforementioned Calvin Murphy is another of the top-ranking foul shooters of the day. Late in 1975, he made 58 free throws in a row, breaking the nineteen-year-old record of 55 held by Bill Sharman.

"Free-throw shooting wasn't something that came naturally," Murphy says. "I had to work and work. Concentration is the key. You have to get a style of your own, stick with it, and concentrate. Then you'll be a good free-throw shooter."

Shooting, of course, is only one of the skills required for success. Passing, dribbling, and rebounding are some others.

Basketball instruction books describe several different types of passes—the two-hand chest pass, jump pass, bounce pass, and baseball pass, to name a few of them. But descriptive names aren't important. The passed ball must be delivered accurately, so that the receiver will be in a shooting position as he catches it. And the speed of the ball has to be appropriate to the situation. Sometimes a lob pass is in order; other times the ball has to be whipped away. If the pass has both of these qualities—accuracy and proper velocity— it doesn't matter how it's delivered or what you happen to call it.

Dribbling the ball, advancing it by bouncing it,

deep breaths. Then the player steps to the line. The referee hands him the ball. Now he has ten seconds in which to shoot. Most players will bounce

Mike Newlin streaks for the basket via a dribble.

In defensive rebounding, you use both hands. This is Spencer Haywood.

used to be much more important to the game than it is today. Not only was dribbling used in setting up shots, but also to kill the clock. Virtually every player was skilled as a dribbler. Of course, players were smaller in those days and, being built closer to the floor, enjoyed a natural advantage as dribblers that a 7-footer can never experience.

Not only has dribbling declined in importance, but it can even be taken as a sign that a team's offense has become sluggish. Coaches want their plays to whip the ball around the court. You can't fast-break when you're dribbling.

This doesn't mean that dribbling doesn't have some value. A player is expected to dribble when there's an unguarded path to the basket, when an opponent has him cornered, when attempting to draw a foul, or any time the offensive situation demands, as in setting up a screen.

While the general level of dribbling has gone downhill, there are, nevertheless, several players active today who are absolute wizards when it comes to deceptive dribbling. One is Pete Maravich of the New Orleans Jazz. Maravich is the master of the behind-the-back dribble, in which he drives toward an opponent while dribbling with his right hand, pushes the ball behind him, then recovers it with his left hand—and without breaking stride.

Maravich can also flick the ball from his right hand to his left between his legs. He can dribble so that the ball bounces with machine gun-like rapidity. He can dribble with his fist instead of his palm. He can dribble with one finger.

While dribbling has somewhat diminished in importance, quite the opposite is true of rebounding. The effort to corral unsuccessful shots that carom off the basket rim or backboard is being pursued more aggressively now than at any other time in the game's history.

How important is a rebound? When the team on the attack gets the rebound, it means another chance to shoot. And considering that pro teams score on almost half their possessions, getting the rebound means a 50 percent chance for two points.

When the defensive team gets the rebound, it prevents the opposition from scoring, and it also sets the stage for its own assault.

There are important differences between defensive and offensive rebounding. In defensive rebounding, a player has to be able to control the ball so he can fire an outlet pass, which triggers the fast break. This means he has to use two hands.

A skilled player will be thinking about the pass even before he goes up for the rebound. As he's jockeying for position underneath, attempting to screen out his opponent, he'll glance toward each side of the court to see where his teammates are positioned. When he leaps for the ball, he has a good idea of where he's going to pass it. Ideally, he will make his pass even before he's landed back down.

On the offensive board, a gentle tap may do the trick. Mitch Kupchak demonstrates.

55

John Gianelli and Elvin Hayes grapple for position.

As soon as the pass is in the hands of a teammate, the defensive rebounder becomes an offensive player. He's got to hurry down the floor. Usually he's the trailer on the break, the man who will get the ball for an outside jump shot should the players up front miss the lay-up. He can also use his momentum to slice through to the boards to attempt a tap-in.

In offensive rebounding, the idea is to score, which can frequently be accomplished with one hand, that is, by tapping the ball in. Of course, you can't tap the ball unless you're close to the rim or backboard. But getting in close is a struggle because a defensive player is trying to box you out. The result is a pushing and shoving match. Hammering hips and flying elbows are common. The area under the basket is sometimes called a "butcher shop."

Leaping ability is also the basic skill required in any jump-ball situation. A jump is used to open the game. In such cases, it's called the tip-off.

A jump ball is also used to put the ball in play in a variety of other situations, such as when two opposing players have possession of the ball simultaneously, or when the ball goes out of bounds after being touched simultaneously by two opposing players, or when a clean block is made on the ball and the shooter comes down with it in both hands. A jump is also used in those rare cases when the ball lodges between the rim and the backboard following a shot.

"Jump ball," signals referee Norm Drucker.

Right: Celtics' Dave Cowens (foreground) duels Harvey Catchings of the 76ers on a jump ball.

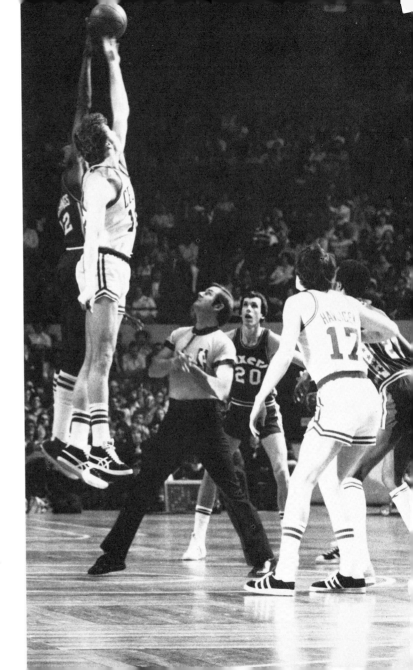

Although not tall, Calvin Murphy can get up high.

The players that do the jumping are not permitted to tip the ball while it's still on the way up. Sometimes a player will sneak an illegal tip and get away with it. But the majority depend on their leaping ability and a keen sense of timing to be successful.

Strategy is also involved. Teams have jump plays in which the jumper attempts to tip the ball to a specific teammate, while the other players break for the basket. The jumper doesn't slap the ball, but merely flicks his wrist to gently bat it.

Sometimes a mismatch will occur. A small guard will have to jump against a big center, a Mike Riordan against a Nate Thurmond. The smaller man may try to crowd his opponent, so as to get a positional advantage. But his team will usually concede that he is not going to win the duel, and will set up a defensive play.

Not being tall is a big disadvantage, and not just in jump-ball situations. The average forward in the NBA is 6-foot-7. To be less than that is to penalize yourself any time you shoot or rebound.

Yet some players manage to succeed in pro basketball without being exceptionally tall. Calvin Murphy, who stands 5-foot-9½ and weighs 165, is the most notable of basketball's "small" men.

"Never in my wildest dreams, not even when I was a cocky kid, could I ever see myself where I am now," Murphy once recalled. "I used to go to Madison Square Garden in New York, and I saw Oscar Robertson's first game there. I daydreamed I

Monte Towe, the game's smallest player.

was out there checking Oscar Robertson and all that, but I never really thought it was possible until my junior year of college." Murphy, who was born and brought up in Norwalk, Connecticut, was a college star at Niagara University.

Murphy's go-go-go style of play not only enabled him to make the grade in the pros, but rendered him one of the key members of his team, the Houston Rockets. He led the club in both scoring and assists in 1975-76. "I try to drive in to the basket as much as possible," he says, "because it makes the defense come to me. When it does, it's got to leave someone open.

"All my life I heard about the disadvantages of being small, but I've discovered there are advantages, too. I can squeeze through mouse holes. That's my way. I've got to get up and go over."

Murphy is not *the* smallest player in the NBA. Monte Towe, a guard with the Denver Nuggets beginning in 1975, is. He stands, he says, 5-foot-6¾. Towe was the smallest player on his team at Oak Hill High School in Converse, Indiana, but it didn't prevent him from being named to the state's All-Star team in his senior year.

At North Carolina State, he was again the smallest man on the squad. "My size," Towe once told sportswriter Mike Lupica, "stands out in the pros more than it did in college. But," he added with a grin, "I prefer to think of myself as being surrounded by abnormal people."

ON THE ATTACK

"At times we approach the ideal of how the game should be played. When one of us moves, the others adjust. We have unselfishness, cooperation, technique. We hit the open, move without the ball, and help out on defense. Everybody is moving, helping out on every play."

That's how guard Bill Bradley described the New York Knicks in 1973, a year the team won the NBA title. What Bradley said can be summed up in one word: teamwork. It's probably more important in basketball than in any other sport.

Year in and year out, the championship is won by the team that plays the best together. The game's biggest "names" sometimes never get beyond the first playoff round.

Every player wants to shoot. "Going for the numbers," it's called. Wanting to shoot is as natural as wanting a drink of water in the fourth quarter. But the impulse to shoot has to be resisted by any player who does not have a "good" shot; otherwise, the team is likely to wind up the season with one or two very high scorers and a big total of losses.

There are more than a few observers who believe that the unselfish player, the team player, is becoming a rare breed in professional basketball. Players want to be individualists today, as one can judge by counting the number of off-balance, out-of-position shots that can be seen in the average game.

Scott Wedman gets applause for his team play.

NBA champions in 1976, the Boston Celtics, here with general manager Red Auerbach, were a team that blended many different skills. They had (left to right) guard Jo Jo White, the team's playmaker, the man who orchestrated the fast break; guard John Havlicek, hustling, aggressive, with the ability to drive or pop from the outside; forward Charlie Scott, a sharpshooter; forward Paul Silas, a ferocious rebounder; and center Dave Cowens, also an excellent rebounder, very mobile, and with the stamina to run all night.

There are exceptions, of course. Bill Bradley of the Knicks was one player who resisted the trend. Among young players, Kansas City's Scott Wedman and Golden State's Jamaal Wilkes think and act more for the good of the team than for themselves.

The reason that teamwork is so important has to do with players' assignments, which are more fluid in basketball than in any other sport. In football, for instance, a linebacker never catches passes or carries the ball (unless he intercepts or recovers a fumble). A center doesn't kick field goals. But in basketball, players move anywhere on the court and take part in all the action. When a team is in possession of the ball, the players work to score. When the opposition gains possession, the same players assume defensive roles.

A coach strives to put together a five-man starting unit that will be a "team" in the fullest sense of the word. When it comes to forwards, a coach wants one forward who can shoot and score and also perform capably as a rebounder. Elvin Hayes of the Bullets and Rick Barry of the Warriors are forwards of this type. At the other forward slot, a coach will look for more of a defensive player, a rebounding specialist. The classic player of this type was Dave DeBusschere of the New York Knicks.

More and more forwards cast in the DeBusschere mold are coming into the pro game. Bob Love of the Chicago Bulls, Rudy Tomjanovich of the Houston Rockets, and Aaron James of the New Orleans Jazz, all of whom stand 6-foot-8, are not simply forwards in the traditional sense; they are *power* forwards, valued as much for their ability to rebound as to score.

The role of the so-called "small" forward, the quick, running forward, typified by such players as John Havlicek of the Celtics and Bill Bradley of the New York Knicks, both of whom stood 6-foot-5, may be diminishing. "The problem with the small forward is that you can take advantage of him and force mismatches underneath," Dick Motta, coach of the Bulls, points out.

The guards have to have balance, too. One will

Rudy Tomjanovich (foreground) typifies the forward who can rebound as well as shoot.

be a shooting guard, a player who is able to put the ball in from the outside as well as drive. He also has to be skilled as a playmaker. The Celtics' Jo Jo White probably combines all of these skills as well as or better than anyone else. The other guard's responsibilities are primarily defensive. He is usually taller than the shooting guard, has excellent mobility, and is also skilled as a playmaker. Fiery Norm Van Lier, a favorite of fans of the Chicago Bulls, excels as a guard of this type.

When it comes to his center, if a coach had his choice, he would undoubtedly pick a player such as the Lakers' Kareem Abdul-Jabbar. He is tall and agile. He can score from underneath or from the top of the key, the free-throw area. He controls the boards. Simply stated, he takes charge. A second type of center is represented by Dave Cowens of the Celtics and Alvan Adams of the Suns. They're not quite as tall as the Abdul-Jabbar type, but they're more mobile and more accurate from the outside. They mesh better with a fast-breaking offense.

Rarely is a coach able to obtain players that fit the above descriptions perfectly. So they work with the players they do have, developing a blend they hope will be successful.

What happened to the Los Angeles Lakers in the 1975-76 season is clear proof as to the importance of having a balanced team. Before the season began, in the biggest trade in the history of the game, the Lakers obtained Kareem Abdul-Jabbar,

John Gianelli sets a pick for Bill Bradley. Charlie Scott is the victim.

the best player in pro basketball at the time. The Lakers were promptly picked to capture their division title and perhaps take the league championship as well. But the team finished next to last in the division standing and never even won a playoff berth.

The Lakers' poor showing was not the fault of Kareem. He finished second in scoring in the league, averaging slightly more than 27 points a game. He led the league in rebounding, hauling down more balls than he ever had before. He had more assists than in any other season and he led the league in blocked shots. He was named the NBA's Most Valuable Player.

What did happen then? Abdul-Jabbar had a supporting cast that didn't support him very well. The guards, Gail Goodrich and Lucius Allen, lacked in ball handling and defensive skills. Goodrich was strictly a shooter. Allen liked to shoot, too, but was inconsistent. The forwards, Cazzie Russell and rookie Don Ford, could put the ball in the basket, but seldom gave a thought to defense.

Any team that has an Abdul-Jabbar in the lineup has championship potential. But the man cannot make a team a winner by himself.

Pro teams also have what is known as a "sixth man," one of the reserve players who comes in from the bench to relieve a tiring starter. John Havlicek, before he attained a starring role with the Celtics, was Boston's sixth man, the best in the game, in fact, triggering rallies with his explosive play. Like many of basketball's super substitutes, Havlicek could play at either the guard or forward positions.

Being a sixth man is no easy task. He is expected to go at full speed from the moment he steps out onto the floor. He has to get points right away. He can't pace himself as other players do.

The offensive system a team uses depends on the type of personnel a team has. The fast break is the best known method of attack. Players simply attempt to outrace the opposition to the basket.

Not every team can stress the fast break. It requires a center and guards who can get the rebounds (because you can't fast-break if you don't get the ball) and have plenty of stamina. Big centers are sometimes deficient in this regard. Dave Cowens of the Boston Celtics is an exception. He's one center who can pound up and down the court all night long, and he's also a demon rebounder. Naturally, the Celtics are a fast-breaking team.

Other teams put more of a stress on set plays. But set plays are rarely as important in pro basketball as they are in college or high school play. The reason is the 24-second clock, which puts a time limit on shooting. In other words, there's not always sufficient time to get each player "set" in his proper position and then work the ball to the designated shooter.

As Darryl Dawkins gathers in the rebound, his fast-breaking Sixer teammates begin to surge upcourt.

In the years that Kareem Abdul-Jabbar spent with the Milwaukee Bucks, 1969-1975, they were the most "play-minded" team in the game. Coach Larry Costello installed about 100 different plays, and in virtually everyone of them Kareem was the designated shooter. Knowing that Kareem was going to end up with the ball most of the time, the opposition would double-team him, and he would have to struggle and strain from the beginning of the game to the end. He might get as many as 20 or 25 points in the first half, but he'd often be so fatigued by the final period that he might score only four or five points. It was generally believed that the Bucks might have been more successful had Costello relied more on the instincts of his players and their ability to improvise, rather than forcing them to adhere to carefully drawn diagrams.

The Chicago Bulls use a much different strategy, running only a few plays. Their offense is based on setting screens inside and quick cuts to the basket. Timing and tenacity are the hallmarks of their game.

The Boston Celtics have a total of about eight plays that they rely upon, and each has several variations. The plays are not complex, involving only a single pass and cut. Or a play will feature a crisscross that forces a mismatch.

To call a play, voice and hand signals are used. "Three! Three!" the Celtics' Jo Jo White will call out, or he'll hold up two fingers in a "V for Victory"

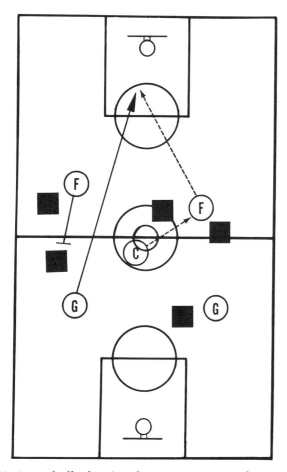

This jump-ball play involves a screen. As the center taps the ball to the forward on the right side, the other forward screens for the guard on the left side. As the guard darts for the basket, the forward hits him with a pass.

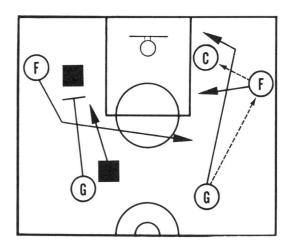

This play has the center in a low post position. The guard on the right passes to the forward, who passes to the center. Both the guard who originated the play and the forward then cut off the center for a possible pass. The guard on the other side sets a screen for the forward, who cuts to the right side to give the center another passing option.

sign. Some teams use a letter of the alphabet to call their plays, or perhaps the name of a city. If the Pistons develop a clever play and some other team copies it, that team might call the play "Detroit."

Plays are frequently called to exploit a particular player. Suppose the Celtics are playing the 76ers, and George McGinnis is in foul trouble. Naturally, the Celtics want to get McGinnis out of the game. So they're likely to call a play that has Dave Cowens, their big pivotman, driving on McGinnis. McGinnis is going to have to go nose-to-nose with Cowens in an effort to prevent the shot, risking another foul, or simply conceding him the basket.

Set plays frequently involve the center, who sets up either a "low post" or "high post." The low post position is close to the basket, to either side of the boards and just outside the free-throw lane. The high position is farther back, at about the top of the free-throw circle.

A center who prefers the low post—Kareem

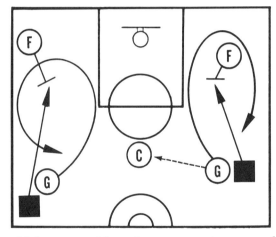

In a high post position, the center gets a pass from the guard on the right side. The guard then circles to his right, and cuts back toward the center for a possible pass. The forward sets a pick. The same type of action is taking place on the other side of the court, giving the center two passing options.

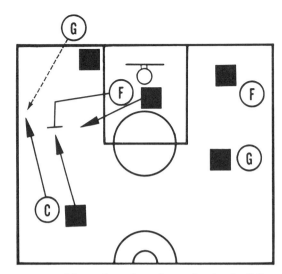

Here a guard is assigned to throw in the ball from in back of the end line. As he takes possession from the referee, the center darts forward to pass. The forward sets a pick to clear his path.

Abdul-Jabbar is one—is likely to be taller than the average center, and he'll be extremely accurate at close range. The low post enables him to get close to the basket for bank shots and rebounds.

A center who sets up at the high post will be a good outside passer. He'll set up with his back to the basket and pass off to his teammates, who go sluicing by him on either side. He'll be skilled at screening, too.

Teams also use two or three jump-ball plays and several out-of-bounds plays. In an out-of-bounds situation behind a team's basket, the play will usually designate a man inside to get the ball, but there will also be a "safety valve" man designated, a player who is positioned deep and is almost certain to be open. The ball will go to the deep man if the in-bounds man is tightly covered and the five seconds allotted a team to complete the play is threatening to run out.

The team on defense will harass the man throwing in the ball, attempting to cut off his passing lanes. And the team will also closely cover the man he's targeting on. If the defensive coverage is so efficient that the in-bounds man can't spot an open

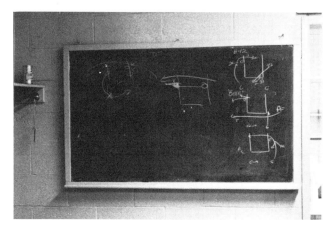

Coach Tommy Heinsohn diagrammed these plays for the Boston Celtics during halftime break.

man, he's likely to call a timeout rather than risk a turnover.

Every team has one or two special plays to rely upon in the last seconds of a game when a basket will tie the score or provide the winning edge. The play is usually designed to get the ball to the team's most reliable scorer.

A team will try to make the final basket of the period with about three seconds remaining on the clock. Then the opposition doesn't have sufficient time to do anything but make a desperate scoring attempt, perhaps firing the ball the full length of the court.

But the strategy can be more sophisticated. Suppose the Lakers are playing the Warriors. The

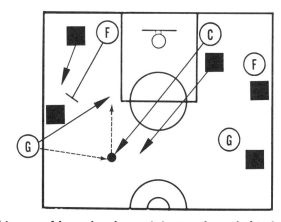

This out-of-bounds play originates from behind the sideline. The guard passes to the center, who darts up for the ball; then the guard takes a return pass and drives for the basket for a lay-up. The forward sets a pick for the guard so he'll have a clear path.

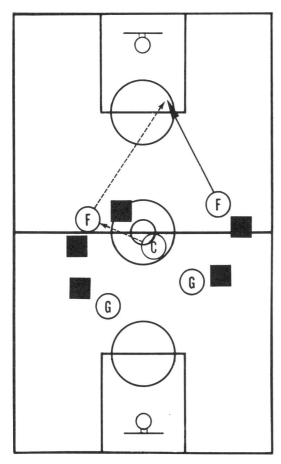

In this jump-ball play, the center taps the ball to the forward on the left side. At the same time, the other forward breaks for the basket. He gets the pass and drives in for a lay-up.

Lakers will try to get a shot away with 33 or 34 seconds left in the quarter. If the shot is good, the Warriors get the ball. Since the Warriors have to shoot within 24 seconds, the Lakers will get the ball back with plenty of time remaining to try for still another basket. Perhaps they'll have as many as 14 or 15 seconds. What it boils down to is that the Lakers get the last two-out-of-three scoring opportunities of the quarter.

Besides the fast break and the use of set plays, a team might emphasize one-on-one strategy, relying on clever passing and feinting to free a particular player for an easy shot. A team using this strategy never stops moving in its effort to set up a mismatch. It might involve a tall man being guarded by a shorter man, a fast man vs. a slower man, or a clever ball handler matched against one who is not so clever.

The one-on-one style requires a player with moves, a player such as Julius Erving—Dr. J. He'll drive toward an opponent, fake one way, fake another, move his head, move a hip, fake a shot, fake another shot—then bang! It's two points. For sheer dazzle, no other player is quite the equal of the good Doctor.

Dr. J is only a fair outside shooter and he will never win any All-League nominations for the way he plays defense, although he has improved steadily in both of these areas since becoming a professional in 1971. He gets high marks for his dribbling. He is

smart and accurate as a passer. He's outstanding as a rebounder.

But what makes Erving special is his ability to do things with the ball that no one else can do. He handles the ball the way the average person handles a grapefruit. He can reach *down* with one hand and snatch the ball away from an opponent's grasp. He can pluck a pass out of the air the way a first baseman gloves an infield throw. He can also jump higher than any one in the game, and can hang in the air while those who have jumped with him have already returned to the floor.

Once, in a game against the Denver Nuggets, Erving was being guarded by Bobby Jones, one of the best defenders in the ABA. Erving scored every time he touched the ball in the first six minutes of play. Each basket came on a drive, but each was distinctly different. The first was on a dunk, the Doctor soaring straight in for the hoop. The next time he scored he eased the ball gently off his fingertips. Then he drove around Jones and curled the ball in from the right side. For his fourth basket, he drove left and scored on a reverse lay-up. Then he tried the right side again and ended with another reverse lay-up.

Jones fouled him as he scored the fifth basket, and the Doctor added a free throw. It all added up

Dr. J first won national acclaim as a member of the New York Nets.

to 11 points in six minutes.

Julius is just a shade less than 6-foot-7, but his hands and feet could belong to a much bigger man. He wears a size 13½ glove and a size 15 sneaker. "His greatness is in his big hands," said Kevin Loughery, who coached Julius in the three seasons that he spent with the Nets. "There are several pros with hands as large, but none have his size, strength, and sensitivity. If he can get a couple of fingertips on the ball, he'll control it."

Players such as Dr. J are in very short supply, of course. Teams, instead, must rely upon more conservative offensive tactics—fast-breaking, using set plays, or a combination of both.

But no matter what strategy is used, the players have to work together. Success depends on timing, movement, and precision passing. Success depends on teamwork.

When he joined the 76ers, Dr. J switched to No. 6.

THE BIG MAN

The Lakers have Kareem Abdul-Jabbar, who is 7-foot-1⅞ (by his own testimony). The Bulls have Tom Boerwinkle, and the Bucks, Elmore Smith, both of whom are 7-footers. In Philadelphia, there's Darryl Dawkins, 6-foot-11, the same height as Bob Lanier of the Detroit Pistons.

Every team today has its big, ball-hawking center. But in basketball's early days, there were no exceptionally tall men, never any 7-footers. It was rare, in fact, for a player to be as tall as 6-foot-6. Joe Lapchick, who played for the Original Celtics for thirteen years beginning in the 1922-23 season, was considered a "giant." Lapchick was 6-foot-5.

Men of Lapchick's height were treated rudely by the rulesmakers. A favorite tactic was for the tall man to station himself close to the basket, hold the ball high above his head, and keep it there until he could turn and make his shot. To put a stop to this, the three-second rule was adopted in 1932. This prohibited a pivotman from standing motionless with the ball, his back to the basket, for more than three seconds. Later the rule became more inclusive, preventing *any* offensive player, with or without the ball, from staying in the "lane" between the foul line and the basket for more than three seconds.

Bob Lanier is Detroit's "big man."

During the same period, the 10-second rule was adopted. This was intended to prevent a team with a big lead from "freezing" the ball, that is, keeping possession without making any attempt to score. The 10-second rule established a line at midcourt. The team in possession had to bring the ball into the front half of the court within the space of 10 seconds.

The tall man's superiority was cut again in 1937. Up to that time, there had always been a tip-off—a center jump—after each basket. This rule caused no problem when teams were about equal size. But when one team happened to have a very tall man who could jump, that team enjoyed an enormous advantage. Every time his team scored, it was very likely to wind up in possession of the ball again. So the rulesmakers eliminated the center jump, except at the beginning of each quarter. (Today, there's a center jump only at the beginning of the game.)

Instead of a jump, the ball was given to the team that had just been scored upon. While the tall man could still get a lion's share of rebounds and usually was able to outscore his shorter rivals, he no longer could use his height to indefinitely gain possession of the ball for his team by means of an unending series of jump balls.

World War II did much to popularize the use of tall men. The military draft took most "normal"-sized players, so coaches had to rely on whatever remained. In baseball, this led to the use of a one-armed outfielder. His name was Pete Gray and he played for the St. Louis Browns. Professional football turned to scores of aged or physically deficient players, men who normally would have been bench warmers—or spectators. Basketball teams, in many cases, began using the draft-exempt tall man.

There were deep-seated prejudices against such men at first. They were considered to be poorly coordinated, and awkward and slow as a result. Often they were called "goons."

Bob Kurland was the first tall player to come to national prominence, although he never played professional basketball. From St. Louis, where he attended Jennings High School, Kurland arrived at the campus of Oklahoma A&M in Stillwater in 1942. He was seventeen years old and 1½ inches short of 7 feet. "I remember," Hank Iba, his coach, once recalled, "when I brought Kurland to New York's Madison Square Garden as a freshman. The other coaches looked at him and said, 'Henry, you'll never make a basketball player out of that guy; he's too tall.'"

The coaches were quickly proven wrong, of course. After Kurland learned to leap so high that his elbows cleared the basket rim, Iba made a goalie out of him, posting him near the basket to block shots, his role similar to that of the goaltender in ice hockey. So successful was Kurland that during his sophomore year the National Collegiate Athletic Association passed the rule forbidding goaltending.

Bob Kurland led Oklahoma A&M to NCAA championship twice, then starred for Phillips Oilers.

No longer could a defensive player touch the ball when it was on or directly above the basket rim. The rule prevails in pro basketball today.

This scarcely affected Kurland, however. Oklahoma A&M won the NCAA championship in 1945 and again in 1946, Kurland's junior and senior years. Never before had a team won the college title two years in a row. Kurland was an All-American both years.

After graduation, Kurland, an A student, was undecided about joining the professional ranks. The pro game was just getting started and teams were not known for their financial stability. For a time Kurland was interested in joining a team called the St. Louis Bombers. "I suppose they'd have given me anywhere from $15,000 to $18,000 a year," Kurland recently recalled. "At least, they promised me that much. But I wasn't sure they would stay solvent." Instead of turning professional, Kurland joined the Phillips Petroleum Company to play industrial-league basketball with the firm's Phillips 66 Oilers.

Kurland was paid the salary of a graduate engineer and considered an amateur. He was thus chosen for the U.S. Olympic team in 1948 and 1952. The Americans were gold medalists both years. Kurland had the honor of carrying the United States flag in the closing ceremony of the 1952 Olympics, which marked the end of his basketball days.

Kurland's career paralleled that of another tall

George Mikan, big and bruising. In his time he was "Mr. Basketball."

man—George Mikan. But Mikan did choose to become a professional rather than continue as an amateur, and the decision helped to make him a well-known figure. When, in January, 1951, the Associated Press polled 380 writers and broadcasters to determine whom they considered to be the finest basketball player in the first half of the twentieth century, Mikan finished first in the voting. He was "Mr. Basketball" of his time.

Mikan was 6-foot-10; he weighed 250 pounds. As these statistics may suggest, he was as brawny as he was tall. Indeed, his style of play had a brutish quality about it. When he whirled his hook shot toward the hoop, anyone in the way was likely to end up on the floor.

Blood often flowed when Mikan was playing— and it wasn't always the opponent's. In his first game Mikan lost four teeth, a mishap quite mild compared to others that were to befall him. He also suffered a broken nose, a broken wrist, two broken feet, four broken fingers, and cuts requiring 166 stitches.

Mikan's first contact with the sport was as a young boy in his hometown of Joliet, Illinois. His father laid out a crude basketball court in the back of the Mikan house. There George and his friends had their rough-and-tumble basketball games, his grandmother serving as referee and enforcing her decisions with a broomstick.

One day during a game George accidentally

stepped on the ball and fell and broke a leg. Doctors predicted that he would never play basketball again. For a time, George must have agreed with them. His high school coach found him to be too big and clumsy, and he failed to make the school team.

George had his heart set on becoming a priest and wanted to attend Notre Dame. He still felt that basketball offered him his best chance of getting an education. But when he sought a scholarship, the Notre Dame coach said that he would never make it as a basketball player, that he was too slow and heavy.

So George enrolled at DePaul University in Chicago. There his tallness and his brawniness were not considered shortcomings. Even the fact that he had to wear thick eyeglasses because of nearsightedness did not seem to make any difference. The DePaul coach had George's eyeglass frames fitted with nonshattering lenses and had him tape the glasses to his temples. Countless times in the years that followed, flailing elbows were to jam the eyeglass frames against his face, causing painful cuts, many of which required stitches.

Mikan was supreme in the four years that he played for DePaul, setting all kinds of scoring records. He was an All-American choice in 1944, 1945, and 1946, and in two of those years he was named "Player of the Year."

As a professional, he enjoyed even greater success. He signed with the Chicago American Gears of the National Basketball League (not the National Basketball *Association*) in 1946. The NBL had been in operation since 1937. George received a $25,000 bonus and a five-year, $60,000 contract, making him the highest paid pro player in history up to that time.

But Mikan's greatest fame came as a member of the Minneapolis Lakers, an NBL team that obtained Mikan's contract in 1947. The Lakers won the NBL championship in 1947-48, with Mikan leading the league in scoring and earning the league's Most Valuable Player award. When the Lakers became members of the Basketball Association of America for the 1948-49 season, the hook-shooting Mikan began making basketball history. (The Basketball Association of America was renamed the National Basketball Association in 1949.) He led the Lakers to five NBA championships over the next six years, earning the league's scoring championship and winning all-NBA honors in each of those six years. In the 1948-49 season, Mikan posted a 28.3 points-per-game average, extraordinary for the day. He was the first player in NBA pro playing to score 10,000 points.

After the 1955-56 season, in which he finished fourth in scoring, Mikan decided to retire. "It wasn't a sudden decision," he said. "I had been thinking about it for some time. I've got three boys and they scarcely know me as a father." By this time,

Mikan had a law degree. He took up law practice and entered politics. His name was in newspaper headlines again in 1967 when he agreed to serve as the first commissioner of the newly formed American Basketball Association.

Neither Mikan or Kurland did very much to establish the tall man as a well-coordinated physical specimen, as a real athlete. They could shoot over smaller men; they could outrebound them. But they had some failings. They were slower than the average player and, at times, ungainly and inept, although Mikan could overcome these deficiencies with his enormous power.

"Lumbering" was the word frequently used to describe the game's big men until the gifted Bill Russell arrived on the professional scene in 1956, a rookie with the Boston Celtics. The thin and wiry Russell, just a hair or two shorter than 6-foot-10, used his height differently than any of the tall men who had preceded him. He is generally regarded as the greatest rebounder the game has known. But it is not for his rebounding that Russell is most renown. It is, instead, for his ability as a shot blocker. Not only did Russell block the shots of the man he was assigned to cover, he also blocked shots by those he wasn't covering. Kareem Abdul-Jabbar and Bob Lanier and Elvin Hayes and some other players do that today, but before Bill Russell it was virtually unthinkable. Like Hank Luisetti, who had such a profound effect in shooting styles, Bill Russell revolutionized basketball's defensive game.

The son of an Oakland, California, shipyard worker, Bill almost didn't play basketball at all. His brother had been an outstanding schoolboy athlete, and Bill, believing that he could never equal his brother's accomplishments, decided not to try. One day the high school basketball coach stopped Bill and said, "You're a big boy; why don't you come out for the team?"

"I couldn't make the team," Bill answered. "Those fellows are better than I am."

The coach looked at Bill for a moment, then said, "Son, if you think they're better—they are." Then he turned and walked away.

After that incident, Bill's thinking began to change. He tried out for basketball, made the team, and played as a member of the varsity squad for two years. One day an assistant coach for the University of San Francisco, after watching him play, offered Russell a scholarship. "It was the only scholarship offer I got," Bill once recalled, "so I took it."

Bill led the San Francisco team through two sensational seasons, during which time the club won 55 games in a row and a pair of NCAA championships. Then he joined the Celtics. Boston coach Red Auerbach had his team playing a fast-break, run-run-run game; however, it had never proven successful. The year before Russell signed on with

the club, the Celtics had finished in third place in their four-team division and had been eliminated from the playoff competition in the semifinal round. "I've always been looking for that good big fellow to get me the ball," said Auerbach. "I don't need shooters. Never did. I need that big man."

In Russell's rookie season of 1956-57, the Celtics captured the league championship. They were on their way to winning it again the next season, but Russell injured an ankle during the playoff finals, and the Celtics were beaten by the St. Louis Hawks.

In the years that followed, the Celtics were the dominant team in pro basketball, building a championship record unmatched by any other team in any other sport. From 1958-59 through 1968-69, the Boston team won the NBA title ten times.

Russell, of course, was not the only reason. Bob Cousy, Bill Sharman, Tommy Heinsohn, Sam Jones, and K. C. Jones were some others. Cousy, a pocket-sized guard, was the team's playmaker, leading the league in assists for eight straight years. His flashy dribbling and behind-the-back passes made him the darling of the fans, but his leadership qualities were what endeared him to his teammates. Whenever the situation grew tense, the ball went to Cousy. Sharman was a two-way guard, a scorer as well as a determined defender.

Bill Russell began his career as a shot-blocker while attending the University of San Francisco.

Heinsohn, known as "Gunner" to his teammates, was often the team's leading scorer. He loved to shoot. Once, in an All-Star game, he touched the ball 23 times and shot it 21 times. Heinsohn became the team's coach in 1969. Sam Jones is ranked as one of the finest backcourt men in NBA history. Like Sharman, whom he succeeded, he was a demon scorer. K. C. Jones hounded opposition forwards like a man possessed.

But it was Russell who was the key to the team's success. "All the others—Heinsohn, Cousy, Sharman, the two Joneses—were great ball players," Ed Macauley, who preceded Russell as the team's center, once observed, "but if you had taken any one of them away, the team still could have accomplished everything it did, even though it would have been more difficult. But not if you had taken away Russell. Then it would have been impossible."

Russell had amazing quickness and an excellent basketball mind. His ability to perceive what an opposing team was trying to do or about to do was as much a factor in his success as his physical attributes.

He also had great pride and determination. In 1962, after the team had won its fifth NBA title in six years, someone asked Russell how he was able to account for the fact that he was on so many

Russell leaps to block shot by Philadelphia's Billy Cunningham.

79

winning teams.

"I just don't know how to lose," he said quietly.

Despite his unrivaled success, playing the game was never easy for Russell. He had a nervous stomach and would get sick before games. In the final game of the 1962 playoffs, the Celtics vs. the Lakers, Russell was never better. With the score tied in the game's closing seconds, Russell leaped to block a shot that would have decided the game in the Lakers' favor. And in the overtime period, Russell gathered in two key rebounds that helped to bring the Celtics the title once more. Bill scored 30 points in the game, grabbed 40 rebounds, and ranked as the outstanding player on the floor. When the final buzzer sounded, Russell hurried to the locker room. There he got violently ill and wept uncontrollably.

Toward the end of his career, Russell was once asked how his years of experience benefited him. He smiled. "Now I only get sick before *playoff* games," he said.

Russell took over the coaching reins from Auerbach in 1966 and continued as a player. Philadelphia won the league championship that season. Russell continued as a player-coach for two more seasons, and won the title both times. He joined the Seattle SuperSonics as a coach in 1973.

Some of Russell's most notable performances were those in which he was pitted against Wilt Chamberlain, the greatest scorer the game has

Russell coached Seattle SuperSonics during 1970s.

known. Chamberlain first attracted national attention while attending Overbrook High School in Philadelphia. During his sophomore year, *Sport* magazine featured an article about Chamberlain that was titled, "The High School Kid Who Could Play Pro Ball Now." The colleges bid wildly for Wilt's services. He chose the University of Kansas. But college basketball Wilt found to be something of a bore, and he skipped his senior season to play with the Harlem Globetrotters. After a year with

Chamberlain-Russell duels were classic match-ups.

the Globetrotters, Wilt signed with the Philadelphia Warriors in the NBA.

Before the ink was dry on Wilt's signature, fans and the press were talking about his first confrontation with Russell. Wilt was taller than Russell by slightly more than three inches, stronger, and had a two-inch reach advantage. Their first meeting took place early in November, 1959, at Boston Garden. "We could have sold out Yankee Stadium," Red Auerbach said.

Russell won the tip-off and blocked Wilt's first attempt to score, a fall-away jumper. It may have been the first time that anyone had ever blocked that shot. But after that, the duel was rather a standoff. Russell finished with 22 points; Wilt had 30, but he took 19 more shots. Russell outrebounded Wilt, 35 to 28. The most important statistic of all was in Russell's favor: Boston won, 115-106.

"He's the best rookie I've ever seen," said Russell afterward. "The guy's no freak. By the end of the season, he could be the greatest basketball player of all time. His potential is unlimited; there's no stopping him."

What Russell said proved true. Chamberlain was the league's Rookie of the Year *and* the Most Valuable Player. No one had ever won both awards before. He compiled some startling statistics that season. He averaged 37.6 points per game. "Startling" is the proper word, because the previous record had been 29.2 points per game. He had 1,941

Wilt Chamberlain

rebounds, totaling 200 more rebounds than Bill Russell.

In the years that followed, as Wilt kept topping himself, he devastated the game's record book. In the 1961-62 season, Wilt scored 4,029 points, averaging 50.4 points per game. Both are all-time records.

His most spectacular achievement took place on March 2, 1962, in Hershey, Pennsylvania, when the Warriors faced the New York Knicks, who were winding up a dismal season. Wilt had 23 points at the end of the first quarter, and a total of 41 at halftime. By the end of the third quarter, he had 69 points, and seemed certain to be on his way to breaking his own one-game record of 78 points. In the final quarter, excited fans left their seats to ring the court and cheer Wilt on. Whenever the Warriors got the ball, then fans would chant, "Give it to Wilt! Give it to Wilt!" Any Warrior besides Wilt who attempted a shot was booed loudly.

His teammates got the message, and began passing to Wilt at every opportunity. Wilt's total soared into the 90s in the game's final minutes. With each basket, the fans became more frenzied. When he reached the 100-point mark 42 seconds from the end of the game on a dunk, hysterical fans stormed out onto the court. They mobbed Wilt, grabbing and shaking his hands and clapping him on the back. The scene was repeated at the final buzzer, and it took several minutes before security guards could reach Wilt and escort him to the dressing room.

Wilt became the first player in basketball history to score 100 points in a game that night. Only a dozen or so years before, it would have been con-sidered unusual if an entire team scored 100 points.

As one might expect, the Warriors won the game. The score was 169-147. The total points scored—316—established a record, too. (The record was equaled in 1970.)

Chamberlain weighed about 250 pounds. He worked with weights and was very muscular, and was said to be the strongest man in sports. He had excellent balance and, while no Bob Cousy, could move well.

Bill Russell was about the only player in the league who could cope with him. A reporter once asked Russell what strategy he used against Wilt. "I try to keep him away from the ball and stay between him and the basket," said Russell.

"And what do you do when neither works?" the reporter asked.

"Panic," said Russell with a grin.

While Wilt was to accomplish some undreamed-of feats as an individual, the teams he played for seldom earned championship status. Not until the 1966-1967 season, back in Philadelphia after a two-year sojourn with the San Francisco Warriors, and playing with the 76ers, did Wilt experience the thrill of winning an NBA championship. Interestingly, Wilt scored only half as many points that season as he had in 1960-1961. The difference was that he had a more talented supporting cast, whose skills blended with those of his own.

Not long after, Wilt was dealt to the Los Angeles

To the photographer who took this picture, Chamberlain, in getting up from the floor, "looked like a giant spider."

Chamberlain goes up against Nate Thurmond in 1972 playoff game.

Lakers. That team won the NBA title in 1972. Wilt averaged a mere 14.8 points per game that season. Instead of trying to score, he concentrated on rebounding and playing defense. He finished No. 1 as a rebounder, averaging 19.2 rebounds per game.

Wilt was magnificent in the playoff finals against the Knicks, dominating play from the opening tip. He blocked shots and intimidated shooters when they got in range. And when they didn't get in range, he'd sometimes chase into the corners after them.

"This was one of the most satisfying games I've ever played," said the Lakers' Jerry West after the team's final victory. "For a long while, me and friends of mine would hear, 'Wilt can't win the big ones.' Well, we won't be hearing that any more."

Wilt Chamberlain holds virtually all of the NBA scoring records, but one day they could belong to Kareem Abdul-Jabbar. Not only has he succeeded Chamberlain as the Lakers' center, but he has inherited his role as the dominant player in professional basketball.

In the official NBA record manual, Abdul-Jabbar's height is listed at 7-foot-2. Countless magazine articles have referred to him as being anywhere up to 7-foot-5. What is his actual height? "I'm 7-foot-1⅞-inches." Abdul-Jabbar told Sam Goldaper of *The New York Times* in 1976. "Anyone who says otherwise is fallacious."

Abdul-Jabbar noted that Tom Burleson was

Kareem Abdul-Jabbar

listed as being 7-foot-4 when he played at North Carolina State, but, according to the Seattle Super-Sonics, the team Burleson joined in 1974, he is "only" 7-foot-2½. "Tom Burleson is taller than I am," said Abdul-Jabbar. "I know. I look up to him, and I'm not used to doing that."

Abdul-Jabbar has become preeminent for reasons other than his height. He has strength and stamina. He uses moves, not just muscle.

He can switch from a high post to a low post, or

Abdul-Jabbar isn't resting; this is a muscle-stretching exercise he did before games.

from one side of the lane to the other. He has the agility to bring the ball down the court when called on to do so.

"He could be the first 7-foot backcourt man," said Fred Crawford, his teammate when Kareem played for the Milwaukee Bucks. "He can dribble and make moves no big man ever made before. Bill Russell could dribble straight down the floor, but Kareem can bring the ball up and handle it.

"Offensively, he's a better shot than Wilt Chamberlain. Wilt used to go into the post and lean on people, and when he did, there wasn't much that you could do about it. But Kareem beats you with his speed and agility."

When he was born in New York City on April 16, 1947, Abdul-Jabbar weighed 12 pounds 11 ounces, and was 22½ inches in length. By the time he reached fourth grade, he was the tallest boy in his school, and the school went up to the eighth grade. He was 6-feet tall in sixth grade. One day his teacher looked up from her desk and said to him, "Why aren't you sitting down?"

Abdul-Jabbar is extremely agile; he can move.

"I am sitting down," he replied.

By the end of seventh grade, he had shot up to 6-foot-5. One day he amazed himself during a game by jumping up and touching the basket rim. After the game and when everybody had left, he went out on the gym floor and kept jumping up and touching it. "I did it 30 times in a row just to prove to myself it was no fluke," he says in his autobiography. By the time he was fourteen he stood 6-foot-8 and could dunk the ball.

At Power Memorial High School in Manhattan, Kareem responded to coach Jack Donohue's urging to build his stamina by skipping rope. He also played handball with his father and practiced long hours. He led Power Memorial to 71 consecutive victories. In his three years of varsity play, the team lost one game.

While he was still attending Power, his reputation for being able to dominate a game was such that the National Collegiate Athletic Association legislated against the use of the dunk shot.

No one knows exactly how many colleges tried to recruit Kareem, but it has been said that just about every college north of the Mason-Dixon line —and more than a few south of it—were interested in him to one degree or another. He chose UCLA, then led the Bruins to three consecutive national championships.

Long before he graduated from college, the NBA had reduced the center lane from 16 to 12 feet.

Warming up for an All-Star appearance, Abdul-Jabbar practices a one-hander.

Right: As a rebounder, Abdul-Jabbar had few equals.

That helped Kareem. He couldn't camp underneath the basket and wait for the ball, then lay it up. He had to learn to shoot farther away from the basket,

and he thus developed a greater variety of shots than either Russell or Chamberlain, including an awesome hook shot, known as the sky hook.

Abdul-Jabbar signed with the Milwaukee Bucks after graduating from UCLA. The Bucks' strategy, as dictated by coach Larry Costello, was to work the ball into Kareem in the low post, and then let him wheel toward the basket or pass to an open man. Teams tried several different methods of stopping the Bucks. The Celtics, for instance, made Abdul-Jabbar the sole responsibility of one man— Dave Cowens. The other four Celtic players would then try to control the other four Buck players. This strategy often caused Cowens terrible embarrassment, at least in the early stages of his career, for there were nights that Abdul-Jabbar would score 40 and 50 points against him.

The Cincinnati Royals (the team moved to Kansas City in 1973) tried double-teaming him. "You kind of play it by ear," said Royals' coach Bob Cousy. "One quarter we'll send a double team in from behind. Another quarter from the front. I guess you say we alternate strategy.

"We also get down on our knees and pray. There's just not a lot that you can do."

Kareem was named the league's Most Valuable Player three times in his first six pro seasons, a

Abdul-Jabbar goes over 6-foot-10 Tom Fox with deft hook.

Operating from a high post, Abdul-Jabbar searches for a teammate.

period in which he averaged 30 points per game. Should he continue at that pace and play a full quota of games each season, he would surpass Wilt Chamberlain's all-time scoring record of 31,419 points, in the early 1980s. He led the Bucks to the NBA championship in 1971.

Always serious and sensitive, Abdul-Jabbar has not, by his own admission, led a contented life. He was unhappy with his high school coach and conditions at college. "UCLA was a mistake," he said in his autobiography. He was unhappy with his religion, becoming a Sunnite Muslim, and changing his name. (He was born Lewis Alcindor.) He was unhappy with Milwaukee and the Bucks and forced a trade to the Lakers in 1975.

Los Angeles was something of a disappointment, too. The Laker team he joined was woefully weak at forward and the guards did not see themselves as defensemen very often. The result was that in the 1975-76 season the Lakers did not even make the playoffs. Nevertheless, Abdul-Jabbar impressed his NBA colleagues enough to be voted the league's Most Valuable Player award a fourth time.

The tall and gifted Abdul-Jabbar has to be considered very much of an exception. As a rule, the game's big centers are getting smaller.

The trend started with Wes Unseld of the Washington Bullets. Whatever shortcomings the 6-foot-7½-inch Unseld may have had because of what he lacked in tallness, he made up for with his jumping skill and mobility.

Mobile Dave Cowens, "only" 6-foot-9, may typify the "big man" of the future.

Unseld's rookie season was 1968-69. Two years later, 6-foot-9 Dave Cowens joined the Boston Celtics. Tommy Heinsohn, the Boston coach, was uncertain how to use Cowens at first. Most coaches of the day lived and died by the rule that said a center had to be 6-foot-10 or taller. So Cowens almost became a forward. But when the Celtics did try him as a pivotman, partly at the urging of Bill Russell, Cowens proved devastating as a rebounder and showed that he could move all over the floor.

The Bullets with Unseld came close to two championships but never managed actually to win one. But Cowens led the Celtics to the NBA title in 1973-74, a season in which he was named the league's Most Valuable Player, and he helped the team with the championship again in 1976.

By the late 1970s, there were several other pivotmen cast in the same mold as Cowens and Unseld —Alvan Adams (6-foot-9) of the Suns, Bob McAdoo (6-foot-9) of the Knicks, and Bob Lanier (6-foot-11) of the Pistons.

Being big is no longer enough. Quickness, stamina, the ability to shoot from the outside as well as inside are the skills that are needed today.

ALL ABOUT DEFENSE

"You want to win in this league, you get yourself a big mobile center and a lot of defense," Red Holzman, coach of the New York Knicks, said early in 1976. "Every team has players who can score, so the emphasis has to be on stopping the other fellow.

"Many of the college rookies that are drafted each year by the pros are basically sound. They can run and shoot and have a pretty good idea of what the game is all about. But when we cut them, it's invariably because they can't adjust fast enough to the tougher defense that's played in the pros."

It's true—defense is the key to basketball success. Unless a team plays a tough, tight defense, it seldom will be able to score enough points to win.

Originally, defense was the responsibility of the team's guards. Seldom did a guard venture farther from his goal than midcourt. If he attempted a field goal, it was by means of a long shot. But nowadays every member of a team must be able to play defense.

Good defense requires players who hustle, who concentrate on their assignments, and who are very quick. You can't excel on defense without quickness, without the ability to move with your man, stabbing out with your hands at the ball. Doug

Doug Collins of the 76ers, one of basketball's quickest players.

Collins of the Philadelphia 76ers has been described as the quickest player in the pro game. He once generated so much torsion in whirling to the basket that he tore the sole loose from one of his sneakers.

The 6-foot-6, 180-pound Philadelphia guard says that he became quick by working at it. "In high school," Collins once recalled, "our coach worked us hard on track during the off-season to develop our quickness. We had to run the 440-yard dash. We had to run the high hurdles and run them hard. We had to run cross-country wearing weighted vests."

Collins believes that you can also improve quickness by developing the proper mental attitude. You have to learn to think in positive terms. "If you believe that you can beat a man to a spot, you will—even though you might not have the foot quickness that he has."

Collins prepares for a game by sitting in front of his locker and going into a trancelike state, concentrating on the man he's going to be playing and the man who is going to be playing him. "I try to get in an aggressive frame of mind," he says.

When he comes out on the floor to warm up, Collins runs hard. "I have to really loosen up," he says. "I like to get out of the gate fast. If I get off to a flying start, I'm OK. But if I start slowly, I end up standing around."

Statistics and records make it obvious that Collins has done very little standing around. In 1975-76, his third year with the Sixers, Collins, with a 20.8 points-per-game average, was second only to George McGinnis among Sixer scorers, and he was the team's best foul shooter. But his opponents respected him the most for his ball-hawking skills.

When a man is playing defense, his chief goal is to prevent the man he's guarding from getting the ball. So he'll try to stay between the man and the ball handler, blocking the passing lane.

If the man does get the ball, then the defensive player's tactics depend on the type of player he's guarding. Does the man prefer to shoot or pass? If the man is a shooter, does he prefer to drive or pop from the outside? When he does attempt to penetrate, does he go to the right or left? In other words, a defensive player will know a great deal about each of the opposition players, and react accordingly. Some players keep notebooks filled with information about opposing players.

If a man is an outside shooter, the defensive player crowds him and keeps a hand in his face. The outside shooter needs room in order to get his shot away; you can't give it to him. When a shooter gets in close, the defensive man covers him like a sheet of wallpaper, using his hands, his elbows, his hips, doing anything that's necessary to try to disrupt the shot and make the man give up the ball.

A different set of tactics is used against the driver. You can play back some, so as to cut down

the angle of his drive, even forcing him in a direction he may not want to go. You can also play a passer somewhat loose. The defensive player might even let a passer shoot, knowing that his chances of actually scoring aren't very good.

Walt Frazier of the New York Knicks was rated as one of the best defensive players in the NBA in recent years. When Frazier was guarding an opponent he would always face the man, stationing himself between the man and the basket, or between the man and the ball. Of course, he would know where the ball was at all times, watching it out of the corner of his eye.

Frazier would have studied the man and would know what moves he was capable of. He never watched the man's eyes. He realized that a player could use his eyes to fake a move. Instead, Frazier kept his eyes on the man's belt buckle or chest. When the man attempted a shot, Frazier would go straight up in his attempt to block it. He'd try not to lunge at the man, knowing that he could be guilty of a charging foul.

Frazier had no equals when it came to stealing the ball. He could steal off a dribble or a pass. Frazier's "secret" was that he made it appear as if

Left: Tight guarding by John Gianelli (40) and Walt Frazier (10) thwart Phil Chenier (45) in his effort to pass to a teammate.

Right: John Gianelli leaps to block.

Walt Frazier (right) was loudly praised for his defensive skills.

he was relaxing. "That was my way of 'suckering' a guy in," he once said. "When he sees you looking relaxed, your man might get careless." That's when Frazier would strike, his fingers darting out for the ball, flicking it away.

The team on defense will work to exploit any shortcomings the opposition might have. If there is a poor shooter on the opposing team, then it's likely that he will be the player who winds up with the ball for a clear shot. A slow man will be forced to run. "You can't hide a weak man" is a well-known basketball axiom.

When 5-foot-9 Calvin Murphy joined the professional ranks in 1970, opposition players tried to take advantage of his size—or lack of it. "My first time around the league," Murphy once recalled, "every team we played against would try to force me to play against their biggest backcourt man, and would try to force me to guard him close to the basket. From close range—in their theory anyway —the man could shoot over me with ease."

This piece of strategy is known as "taking a man into the hole." But Murphy would do whatever he had to in order to keep from being drawn into the "hole." He'd scramble and scratch to hold his ground. Eventually teams found out that they had to work so hard to exploit Murphy that they had to disrupt their entire offense. By the end of the season, most teams had abandoned the strategy.

Players' flaws will be turned to the advantage of the defense, too. Even the best pro players have their imperfections. Cazzie Russell of the Lakers, for example, is a poor rebounder. His timing is bad, and he'll sometimes be going up when the ball is coming down, and vice versa. Charlie Scott of the Celtics, a natural right-hander, is consistent with his jumper from the right side. But when he shoots from the left side, he's not able to get it as high in the air, and there's a chance to deflect it. "Force him to the left," say the scouting reports on Scott. Pete Maravich's weak point used to be his very long hair. Just as he stopped dribbling, the hair would settle down over his eyes, and an alert opponent could sometimes steal the ball.

In high school and college basketball, teams use one of two defensive systems: man-to-man or zone. In a man-to-man defense, each man guards a specific player. Wherever that player goes on the court, the defensive man goes, too.

In the zone defense, a player guards a certain area of the court, covering any opponent who enters that area. A team may use both systems in a given game, switching from one to another and back again.

Professional basketball forbids the use of zone defenses. "A zone defense is not permitted in NBA games," the league's official rulebook declares. The rule was put on the books because it was said that the zone slowed down the game to a snail's pace. Dullness was the result. But that was before the 24-

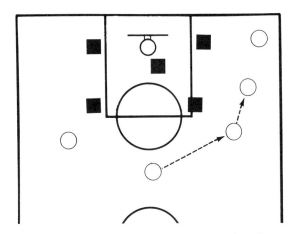

Although illegal, 2-3 zone defense is said to be common in NBA.

second timer was introduced. The zone can't be blamed for slowing down the game any more. But the rule remains in effect.

When a referee judges that a team is using a zone, he issues a warning. If he spots the team using the zone again, the referee calls a technical foul, giving the opposition one foul shot. For every additional violation, another technical foul is called.

Some teams with dominating centers—Los Angeles, with Kareem Abdul-Jabbar, and Portland, with Bill Walton—are frequently accused of using the zone. These men sometimes stay in the lane, regardless of where the man they are guarding goes, and seek to prevent opponents from driving to the basket.

It is generally believed that virtually all pro teams use zone principles in setting up their defense. Some players say that the 2-3 zone is common in the NBA. In this, three players are stretched across the court close to the basket; the other two are to the right and left of the foul line.

Within its basic defense system, a team will use various other pieces of strategy. A team may "press," for instance. To press means to guard the opposition players, particularly the man with the ball, as closely as possible, to really harass him. A full-court press is exactly what the term implies, a press that begins the moment the opposition team takes the ball out of bounds.

A pressing defense is meant to confuse the opposition and force mistakes. It's not an easy defense. Players using it have to be in top-notch physical condition.

Teams also "collapse" or "sag." In a sagging defense, a defensive man will drop off the man he's covering to pick up a player near the basket who is a potential scoring threat. A sagging defense clogs up the middle and, hopefully, forces the offense to take its shots from the outside.

Another defensive tactic is the "switch." Players simply exchange defensive responsibilities when they execute a switch. Suppose Sidney Wicks of the Celtics is guarding Walt Frazier of the Knicks. John Havlicek is guarding Bill Bradley. Frazier has the ball. Bradley sets a pick, screening out Wicks, thus

Double-teamed by eager 76ers, John Havlicek struggles.

leaving Frazier free. So Wicks quickly "switches" with Havlicek and Havlicek moves to cover Frazier as he gets set to shoot. Wicks covers Bradley.

Players are always shouting to one another as they set up their defensive assignments. "Pick! Pick left!" a man will yell. Or you will hear shouts of "Mine! He's mine!" or "Help! I need help!" or "Watch the back door!"

Teams sometimes use the names of colors to designate the character a defense is to take. For example, a coach will yell "Green!" when he wants his players to be aggressive, to press, to take chances and not worry about fouling. A shout of "Red!" can mean he wants his men to play more conservatively, to avoid fouling.

Double-teaming is another frequently used piece of strategy. Suppose the Celtics are playing the 76ers, and the Celtics are on the attack. The ball goes to John Havlicek in the corner. Doug Collins of the 76ers is there to cover him, but forward George McGinnis moves into the corner to help out. Havlicek is now doubled-teamed.

The other 76er players quickly adjust. Forward Julius Erving veers over to cover Celtic guard Jo Jo White. Guard Henry Bibby darts to the top of the key to cover the Celtics' other guard. This leaves forward Sidney Wicks unguarded. But the only way that Havlicek can get the ball to Wicks is by means of a dangerous cross-court pass. You can be sure that every Sixer on the floor is alert for such a pass and a possible interception.

"Team defense," Walt Frazier once said, "is like the pistons on my Rolls. Everything moving smoothly, every guy adjusting, sliding forward and back, depending on the situation."

"THE TRAVEL IS UNBELIEVABLE"

Toward the end of his rookie season in the NBA, David Thompson of the Denver Nuggets, who joined the team in 1975 following a brilliant career at North Carolina State, was asked about the differences between professional basketball and the college version. Thompson didn't mention the pushing and shoving that goes on underneath the boards, the run-run-run style of play, nor the presence of the 24-second timer. "It's the travel," he said. "The travel is unbelievable.

"At college we had 26 games a year, at the most three a week. But in the pros you're playing or flying every day. It's hard to get up for every game."

How much traveling is there? Look at it like this: The NBA season is 82 games in length, not counting the playoffs. An 82-game schedule means 41 games at home, 41 games on the road. And 41 road games mean 41 separate trips in and out of some city. By the third or fourth week of the season, it's become drudgery, a seemingly endless trek from airport to hotel, hotel to arena, and arena to airport.

Sometimes basketball trips can be bizarre. Take what happened to the Golden State Warriors during the 1976-77 season. After a Friday night game against the Spurs, the Warriors boarded a Saturday morning flight from San Antonio for the two-hour trip to Atlanta, where they were to play the Hawks on Sunday. When the airplane arrived over Atlanta,

Marvin Webster hauls luggage through terminal at New York's LaGuardia Field.

Webster pauses to sign an autograph.

weather conditions were such that the plane was not permitted to land. After circling the Georgia countryside for an hour, the pilot decided to proceed to Charlotte, North Carolina, 230 miles to the northeast.

It was midafternoon when the Warriors arrived in Charlotte. At 5:45, after a boring two hours in the terminal waiting room, the players boarded another plane for Atlanta. The same thing happened. Upon arriving over Atlanta, they could not land. This pilot went on to Columbus, Georgia, 110 miles to the southwest.

Upon arrival there, the Golden State trainer, who also served as the team's road secretary, ordered the players off the plane, and tried to rent a bus. But there were no buses available. While the players dined on cheeseburgers at the airport coffee shop, the trainer rented four automobiles. It was 9:30 when the Warrior caravan left Columbus, and they finally got to Atlanta about two hours later. It was almost midnight before the weary travelers had checked into their hotel rooms. The players recovered to beat the Hawks the following night.

Airplane flights are usually made late at night immediately following a game. Or sometimes a team will return to the hotel when the game is over, stay the night, and take a flight early the next morning.

Teams travel in a party of 16 or 17 individuals, including 12 players (the roster limit), the coach, his assistant, the trainer, and perhaps two or three sportswriters. Regularly scheduled airline flights are used, not chartered planes, as in the case of pro football and baseball teams. It's a matter of economics. There are simply too few people involved to make it worthwhile to charter an entire airplane.

Basketball teams have no equipment manager, either, and players are responsible for their own luggage, which usually consists of a garment bag containing a suit, or sports jacket and slacks, a duffel bag provided by the club for uniforms, sneakers, sweat pants, and other playing equipment, plus a small suitcase.

A chartered bus meets flights and brings the team from the airport to the hotel. After arriving at the hotel, some players go to their rooms, others to the coffee shop or a restaurant for a meal, and still others to establishments where strong beverages are available. Do players live it up on the road? Some do. But most coaches have an attitude toward misconduct that is similar to that of Al Attles, coach of the Golden State Warriors. Attles always requests a hotel suite away from the players. "I don't want to know what they're doing," he says. "Frankly, if a guy wants to shorten his career by the way he acts, that's up to him. But we really don't have too many guys who like to kick up the sand."

Suppose a team arrives in a city in the early morning hours for a game that night. By noon, most members of the team are up and will have ordered

On arriving at hotel, players unload their baggage.

breakfast. About four or five hours before the game, players have lunch. It might consist of a soup and salad; nothing heavy. The biggest meal of the day comes after the game. Players are allotted $25 a day in expense money for meals.

"Seldom are two consecutive days the same as far as meals are concerned," says Monte Towe of the Denver Nuggets. "It depends on where you're playing. It depends on what time you get there, when the game is scheduled, and what time the plane is leaving."

Some players may spend their afternoons lazing around the hotel room, watching television or napping. "What you do depends on the city to some extent," says Monte Towe. "In New York or Los Angeles, there's a lot to do and a lot of things you want to see. Some guys will go shopping for clothes. Others have friends they want to see. Or there may be an interview you have to do."

By mid-afternoon, each of the players is beginning to think about the game ahead, about whom he will be guarding and who will be guarding him. He'll have scanned the sports pages of the local newspaper for information about the team—who's shooting well, who's not, and who may be injured.

About two hours before the game is to begin, a chartered bus arrives at the hotel to take the players to the arena. They amble aboard, each carrying his duffel bag.

In the locker room, players take their time getting

dressed for the game. If they're playing at home, there is mail waiting for each man. Perhaps a sportswriter wants an interview. At one hour before game time, everybody except the players, the coaches, and the trainer must leave the locker room. Then the coach may talk to the team, using a blackboard to

Dave Cowens unlimbers before a game at Boston.

outline the strategy he wants used.

About twenty minutes before the game begins, the players file out onto the floor to warm up. They practice their various shots, moving slowly and deliberately at first. They'll try some free throws. They'll dribble some to get the feel of the ball. Some players do special exercises to stretch tendons and ligaments.

Then the referees come out and a loud buzzer sounds, signaling the players to go to their respective benches. The lights dim and the public address announcer introduces each team's starting players one by one. Then they play the National Anthem or, if you're in Madison Square Garden, "America the Beautiful."

The referee sounds his whistle, calling the opposing centers to the center circle. It's game time!

As soon as the game is over, the whole process is repeated. Players shower and dress, take the bus to the airport, board the plane, fly to the next city, and take the bus to the hotel. It is tiring; it is boring. To a married player with a family, it can be lonely. But no one has ever said that basketball players aren't well paid for what they endure. Indeed, they are the highest paid of all professional athletes. The average salary in the NBA in 1976 was $107,000.

Documents filed in a Federal suit known as the Oscar Robertson case showed, for example, that Spencer Haywood's contract paid him a total of

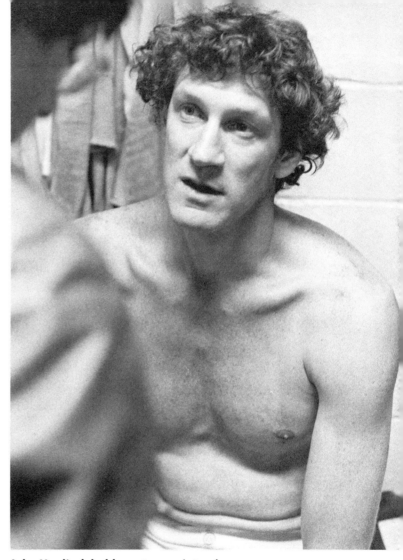

John Havlicek holds postgame interview.

Ziegel on DH:
Page 60

New York Post Sports

64   NEW YORK, THURSDAY, OCTOBER 21, 1976

Pigskin Prophet
On Page 53

Erving: The $6 Million Man

Dr. J's exploits as a negotiator earned him this headline.

$1,510,000 over a five-year period beginning in 1973. John Havlicek earned a million dollars over a four-year span beginning in 1973. Rudy Tomjanovich also earned a million dollars, payable over six years beginning in 1973.

Some players have shown just as much speed and elusiveness in their contract negotiations as they have displayed on the court. Julius Erving has shown more. The Doctor was drafted by the Virginia Squires in March of his junior year at the University of Massachusetts and signed to a three-year, $500,000 contract. During his rookie year with the Squires, Julius began to feel underpaid, and he asked his agent, Bob Wolff, to renegotiate the contract. When Wolff refused, Julius hired another agent.

Not long after, Julius signed with the Atlanta Hawks, but the Squires won him back after a court fight. In the summer of 1973, Roy Boe, owner of the New York Nets, paid off both teams for the opportunity to negotiate with Julius. This time Julius received a $300,000 bonus plus a $250,000-a-year salary.

Dr. J starred for the Nets for three seasons, then began feeling underpaid again. When Roy Boe refused to renegotiate his contract, Julius skipped off to Philadelphia to join the 76ers, who are said to have paid him $3 million for five years of service. (The Philadelphia club also paid the Nets $3 million for the right to sign him.) For such a sum, Julius should be willing to abide the rigors of a good number of road trips.

The hardships of travel weigh more heavily upon very tall players than those of average size. Think of what it is like to be a 7-footer and want to use a telephone booth. Seldom are hotel beds long enough, while the seats in airport coffee shops aren't built far enough from the floor. Sit down and you have your chin on your knees. It's awkward to use bathtubs and showers. Tall players have to be sure to get seats in the first-class section of an airplane. Otherwise, they won't have enough leg room. On the team bus, tall men have to hang their legs over the seat sides into the seat across the aisle.

Automobiles also complicate their lives. Milwaukee center Elmore Smith, a 7-footer, drives a Volvo. But to accommodate his long legs, he has had to adjust the driver's seat so far back that it almost touches the rear seat. And when he turns his head to the left or right, he looks out through the rear window.

Getting clothing that fits can be a struggle. "I wear a size 50 double extra-long sports jacket," says Tom Boerwinkle, the Chicago Bulls' 7-foot center. "Whenever I get in a town, I check out the big-man's store because I might find something. If I do I buy it, even if it doesn't look real good, because there is such a limited selection."

Most players who are Boerwinkle's size have their clothes made. But that can be expensive. A suit costs $250 and up. Trousers are $50 a pair.

Tiny Archibald, who is 6-foot-3, can walk through a hotel lobby or along a city street and

Celtic coach Tommy Heinsohn dispenses autographs to fans at Madison Square Garden.

never be noticed by a soul. But Kareem Abdul-Jabbar can't, nor Tom Boerwinkle, nor any other of basketball's big men. People are always staring, pointing, and whispering about them.

Big men are constantly being asked the question, "How tall are you?" Or people will say, "You're a basketball player, aren't you?" For 6-foot-11 George Johnson of the Warriors, that's the most bothersome question of all. "Don't people think a tall person can do anything else besides play basketball?" he asks. "Don't they think I could be a doctor or a lawyer?"

Another annoying question the tall player hears constantly is "How's the weather up there?" One 7-footer, upon hearing the query for the umpteenth time, is said to have answered by pouring his Coke over the questioner's head and saying, "It's raining."

GLOSSARY

AIR BALL—A shot that misses the basket rim, the net, the backboard—everything.

ALLEY—See Free-throw lane

AMERICAN BASKETBALL ASSOCIATION (ABA)—A professional league that operated from 1967 through 1975.

ASSIST—A pass to a teammate which leads to a score on his part.

BACKBOARD—The 4-foot by 6-foot flat surface to which the basket is attached.

BACKCOURT—That half of the court containing the basket a team is defending.

BACKCOURT FOUL—A foul against a team that is in control of the ball within that half of the floor containing the basket the team is defending.

BASELINE—The line behind the basket which serves as the legal boundary between the playing floor and the out-of-bounds area. Also called the end line.

BASKET—The black metal ring, 18 inches in diameter, with a white cord net, 15 to 18 inches in length, through which the ball is shot in order to score.

BASKETBALL ASSOCIATION OF AMERICA (BAA)—A professional league that was founded in 1946, and renamed the National Basketball Association in 1949.

BLOCKING—A personal foul called when a player illegally impedes an opponent's progress. There is no such thing as a legal block.

BOARDS—The backboard.

BOX OUT—The action of an offensive player in blocking an opponent's path to the play by standing between him and the basket or a teammate.

CENTER—The player who jumps at the center circle against an opposition player at the beginning of each quarter. Also called the pivotman.

CENTER CIRCLE—The 4-foot circle at midcourt.

COLLAPSE; COLLAPSING—See Sag; sagging.

CORNER MAN—See Forward.

COURT—The playing area.

DEFENSIVE BASKET—The basket a team guards.

DOUBLE DRIBBLE—In dribbling, to touch the ball more than once before it touches the floor.

DOUBLE-TEAM—A situation in which two defensive players guard one offensive player.

DRIBBLE—To move the ball by means of repeated bounces.

DUNK—To cram the ball into the basket; to stuff.

END LINE—See Baseline.

FAST BREAK—A quick rush by two or more members

of the offensive team toward the opposition basket.

FIELD GOAL—A two-point score.

FORWARD—One of two players who, with the center, makes up the front line of a team's offense; at the tip-off the forwards line up nearest the team's offensive basket. Also called corner man.

FOUL—Any infraction of the rules.

FOUL OUT—To be disqualified from play for exceeding the number of permissible fouls, which is six in pro basketball.

FOUL SHOT—See Free throw.

FREE THROW—The privilege given to a player to score one point by an unhindered throw from just behind the free-throw line.

FREE-THROW CIRCLE—The 12-foot circle that encloses the foul line.

FREE-THROW LANE—The 16-foot wide area in front of each basket, extending from the baseline to the free-throw line. Also called the alley.

FREE-THROW LINE—The painted line 15 feet from the front plane of the backboard. Free throws are attempted from a point directly behind the line.

FREEZE—To retain possession of the ball without any attempt to score.

FRONTCOURT—That half of the court containing the basket a team is shooting for.

GIVE-AND-GO—An offensive maneuver in which a player passes the ball to a teammate and cuts toward the basket for a pass.

GOALTENDING—A type of interference in which a defensive player touches the ball or basket when the ball is on the basket rim or within the basket itself. Goaltending can also be called if a defensive player touches the ball when it is touching an imaginary cylinder which has the basket rim as its base. If the infraction occurs during a field goal attempt, the offended team is awarded two points; during a foul attempt, one point.

GUARD—One of two players who, at the center jump, lines up farthest from the offensive basket.

HELD BALL—A game situation in which two or more opposing players hold the ball jointly.

HIGH POST—The pivot position taken by the center in which he stations himself in the area of the free-throw circle.

HOOP—The basket or goal.

JUMP BALL—The method used for putting the ball in play following a held ball, a double foul situation, or when both teams cause the ball to go out of bounds, or the ball lodges in a basket support. The referee tosses the ball up between two opposing players.

KEY; KEYHOLE—The entire free-throw area, including the lane and that portion of the free-throw circle beyond the free-throw line. (So-called because it once had a keyhole shape.)

LANE—See Free-throw lane.

LAY-UP—A one-handed, usually banked shot, made close to the basket after a drive.

LEAD PASS—A pass thrown slightly ahead of a breaking teammate.

LOOSE BALL FOUL—A foul committed by a player in pursuit of a free ball or rebound. The offended team is given the ball out of bounds.

LOW POST—The pivot position taken by the center in which he stations himself close to the basket and just to the right or left of the free-throw lane.

MAN-TO-MAN DEFENSE—A type of defense in which each member of the defensive team is assigned to cover a particular player on the opposition team.

NATIONAL BASKETBALL ASSOCIATION (NBA)—A league of 22 professional teams (as of the 1976-77 season), founded in 1946 as the Basketball Association of America. Present name was adopted in 1949.

NATIONAL BASKETBALL LEAGUE (NBL)—A professional basketball league that operated from 1937 through 1948.

OFFENSIVE BASKET—A basket a team shoots for.

OFFENSIVE FOUL—A foul committed by a member of the team on offense. The offended team is given the ball out of bounds.

OUTLET PASS—The pass that triggers the fast break.

OUTSIDE SHOT—Any shot attempted over a long distance.

PALMING—Holding the ball too long at the top of the bounce, a violation of the rules.

PERIOD—One quarter of a game.

PERSONAL FOUL—A foul which involves contact with a member of the opposing team. Blocking, holding, charging, tripping, hacking, etc. are personal fouls.

PICK—A maneuver by an offensive player in which he positions himself so as to block an opponent's path to a teammate with the ball.

PICK-AND-ROLL—A maneuver in which an offensive player moves from a pick position to the basket in anticipation of a pass.

PIVOT—A move by a player in possession of the ball in which he turns either to the left or right, keeping one foot—the pivot foot—at the same point of contact with the floor.

PIVOTMAN—See Center.

POST—The position on the court taken by the pivotman during an offensive play.

PRESS; PRESSING—Tight guarding by the defensive team.

REBOUND—A missed shot that bounces from the backboard or basket rim.

REFEREE—The official in charge of a game. Two referees are assigned to each professional game. The senior referee in terms of length of service is in charge.

SAG; SAGGING—A type of defense in which one or

more players drop off from the men that they are guarding to cover a player or players near the basket.

SCREEN—An action on the part of one player meant to delay or prevent an opponent from reaching a desired position on the floor.

STUFF—See Dunk.

TAP; TAP-IN—A lightly tipped shot off of a rebound.

TEAM FOUL—The extra foul (and free throw) charged to a team once it exceeds the allowable quota of four fouls for a period.

TECHNICAL FOUL—A foul which does not involve contact with a member of the opposing team. It can be assessed not only against a player, but any non-player sitting on the bench, the coach, the assistant coach, etc.

TEN-SECOND RULE—A rule that prescribes that the offensive team, after gaining possession, has ten seconds to bring the ball from its backcourt to its forecourt.

THREE-POINT PLAY—A play that results when a player who scores a field goal is fouled in the act of shooting. If he is successful with the free throw that follows, it results in a third point.

THREE-SECOND RULE—A rule which states that an offensive player cannot remain within the free-throw lane or circle for more than three seconds.

THROW-IN—The method of putting the ball in play from out of bounds.

TIMEOUT—The 90-second interval during which play is halted and the clock stopped.

TIP-OFF—The jump ball between opposing centers that opens a game.

TRAILER—An offensive player who follows a fast break in anticipation of a pass.

TRAVELING—Running with the ball without dribbling it in accordance with the rules. Also called walking.

TWENTY-FOUR-SECOND RULE—A rule which states that a team, after gaining possession of the ball, must attempt a shot to score within 24 seconds. Failure to do so results in loss of possession.

WALKING—See Traveling.

ZONE DEFENSE—A type of strategy in which each member of the defensive team covers a particular area of the court, rather than a specific player. Zone defenses are not permitted in the NBA.

ALL-TIME NBA RECORDS

INDIVIDUAL RECORDS

Most Points Scored, Game

100—Wilt Chamberlain, Philadelphia vs. New York at Hershey, Pennsylvania, March 2, 1962

Most Field Goals, Game

36—Wilt Chamberlain, Philadelphia vs. New York at Hershey, Pennsylvania, March 2, 1962

Most Free Throws, Game

28—Wilt Chamberlain, Philadelphia vs. New York at Hershey, Pennsylvania, March 2, 1962

Most Consecutive Points, Game

15—Wilt Chamberlain, Philadelphia vs. Baltimore at Baltimore, March 20, 1966

Most Rebounds, Game

55—Wilt Chamberlain, Philadelphia vs. Boston at Philadelphia, November 24, 1960

Most Points Scored, Season

4,029—Wilt Chamberlain, Philadelphia Warriors, 1961-62.

Highest Scoring Average, Season

50.4—Wilt Chamberlain, Philadelphia Warriors, 1961-62

Highest Field-Goal Percentage, Season

.727—Wilt Chamberlain, Los Angeles Lakers, 1972-73

Highest Free-Throw Percentage, Season

.932 (367-342)—Bill Sharman, Boston Celtics, 1958-59

Most Rebounds, Season

2,149—Wilt Chamberlain, Philadelphia Warriors, 1960-61

Most Assists, Season

910—Nate Archibald, Kansas City-Omaha Kings, 1972-73

Highest Assist Average, Season

11.5—Oscar Robertson, Cincinnati Royals, 1964-65

Most Personal Fouls, Season

366—Bill Bridges, St. Louis Hawks, 1967-68

Most Disqualifications, Season

26—Don Meineke, Fort Wayne Pistons, 1952-53

Most Steals, Season

288—Rick Barry, Golden State Warriors, 1974-75

TEAM RECORDS

Most Points, Game
173—by Boston vs. Minneapolis at Boston, February 27, 1959

Most Field Goals, Game
72—by Boston vs. Minneapolis at Boston, February 27, 1959

Most Free Throws, Game
59—by Syracuse vs. Anderson at Syracuse, November 24, 1949

Most Consecutive Points, Game
24—by Philadelphia 76ers vs. Baltimore Bullets, March 20, 1966

Most Rebounds, Game
112—Philadelphia vs. Cincinnati at Philadelphia, November 8, 1959
112—Boston vs. Detroit at Boston, December 24, 1960

Most Games Won, Season
69—Los Angeles Lakers, 1971-72

Most Games Lost, Season
73—Philadelphia 76ers, 1972-73

Highest Winning Percentage, Season
.841 (69-13)—Los Angeles Lakers, 1971-72

Lowest Winning Percentage, Season
.110 (9-73)—Philadelphia 76ers, 1972-73

Longest Winning Streak, Season
33 games—Los Angeles Lakers, November 5, 1971-January 7, 1972

Longest Losing Streak, Season
20 games—Philadelphia 76ers, January 9, 1973-February 11, 1973

Most Points Scored, Season
10,143—Philadelphia 76ers, 1966-67

Highest Average Points Per Game, Season
125.4—Philadelphia Warriors, 1961-62

Most Consecutive 100-point Games, Season
77—New York Knicks, 1966-67

Most Games, 100 Points, Season
81—Los Angeles Lakers, 1971-72

Highest Free-Throw Percentage, Season
.821—Kansas City-Omaha Kings, 1974-75

Most Steals, Season
972—Golden State Warriors, 1974-75

Most Division Titles Won
14—Boston Celtics

INDEX